PRAISE FOR

The Sowing Season

"In a world obsessed with instant results, Ashley Hetherington reminds us that faithfulness in the unseen seasons is where real spiritual growth happens. This is a practical and powerful guide to cultivate daily habits that anchor you in God's truth. If you feel stuck, unseen, or tempted to quit, this book will help you stay the course."

—JONATHAN POKLUDA, lead pastor of Harris Creek Baptist Church, bestselling author, host of the *Becoming Something* podcast

"Ashley writes beautifully and intentionally, and she relates to young women through her words in this must-read. *The Sowing Season* will not just challenge you to live in God's best but it will also equip you. If you are a young woman ready to take your faith more seriously and experience God's best, you need this book."

—GRACE VALENTINE, host of the *Water Into Wine* podcast, speaker, and author of *The Better Friend*

"I've had the privilege of watching Ashley live the words she's written in *The Sowing Season*. This book feels like sitting across the table from her with a cup of coffee—honest, encouraging, and full of gentle truth. Ashley reminds us that faith isn't about getting everything right, but it's about showing up, planting small seeds of obedience, and trusting God with the growth. Her words have encouraged me in seasons of waiting, doubt, and hope, and I know they'll do the same for so many others. This book is a gift."

—ARIELLE REITSMA, co-host of the *Girls Gone Bible* podcast and co-author of *Out of the Wilderness*

"*The Sowing Season* is a beautifully grounded and deeply encouraging guide for anyone ready to embrace the power of faithful living in every season of life. Ashley Hetherington's heartfelt wisdom and practical insights help readers discover how small, intentional habits—from prayer and Scripture reading to compassionate friendships and healthy rhythms—can deepen faith and unlock real joy and purpose. With honesty, grace, and spiritual clarity, this book invites us to sow wisely where we are planted and to trust that God's abundant harvest always follows faithful steps. It's a must-read for anyone seeking a closer walk with God and a life marked by meaning and peace."

—ANGELA HALILI, co-host of the *Girls Gone Bible* podcast and co-author of *Out of the Wilderness*

The Sowing Season

The Sowing Season

A PRACTICAL GUIDE TO CULTIVATING SMALL HABITS THAT INVITE GOD'S ABUNDANCE

Ashley Hetherington

WATERBROOK

WaterBrook
An imprint of the Penguin Random House Christian Publishing Group,
a division of Penguin Random House LLC
1745 Broadway, New York, NY 10019
waterbrookmultnomah.com
penguinrandomhouse.com

LIBRARY OF CONGRESS CATALOGING-IN-PUBLICATION DATA
Names: Hetherington, Ashley author
Title: The sowing season / Ashley Hetherington.
Description: First edition. | New York, NY: WaterBrook, 2026 |
Includes bibliographical references.
Identifiers: LCCN 2025040265 (print) | LCCN 2025040266 (ebook) |
ISBN 9780593600719 hardcover | ISBN 9780593600726 ebook
Subjects: LCSH: Spiritual life—Christianity | Spiritual exercises | Hetherington, Ashley
Classification: LCC BV4501.3 .H48 2026 (print) | LCC BV4501.3 (ebook)
LC record available at https://lccn.loc.gov/2025040265
LC ebook record available at https://lccn.loc.gov/2025040266

Printed in the United States of America

1st Printing

First Edition

The authorized representative in the EU for product safety and compliance is
Penguin Random House Ireland, Morrison Chambers, 32 Nassau Street,
Dublin D02 YH68, Ireland, https://eu-contact.penguin.ie

BOOK TEAM: Production editor: Jocelyn Kiker • Managing editor: Julia Wallace • Production manager: Sarah Feightner • Copy editor: Kayla Fenstermaker • Proofreaders: Debbie Anderson, Julia Henderson

For details on special quantity discounts for bulk purchases, contact
specialmarketscms@penguinrandomhouse.com.

Contents

Introduction

Three years ago, I found myself in a slump. I was twenty-four years old, and my brother and I were sharing a rental house—one that my mother owned—in Nashville. I had big hopes and dreams for the future, but my reality was nothing close to what I'd imagined life would look like. Each morning, I woke up to what felt like the same day, with nothing exciting or new happening. I was working toward the dreams and goals God had placed on my heart, but instead of getting closer, my aspirations felt further and further away.

On a typical day I would wake up early and spend time with God while drinking a yummy cup of coffee. Next, I'd get a little work done on my computer, then go to my morning workout. I'd come home, make a healthy breakfast, and get ready for the day. After that, I'd spend the rest of the day writing for my job as a content creator. I'd work with my team to cast vision, edit videos, and create graphics to help women grow in their faith and reach their full potential as children of God. Finally, I'd make dinner, spend time with my brother, and go to bed. *Rinse and repeat.*

I did this every day for weeks on end. Those weeks turned into months. Months turned into years. I realized that no matter how hard I worked and no matter how hard I tried to move on to the next season of my life, I remained exactly where I was.

Despite being obedient to what I felt God was telling me to do and trying my best to be faithful every single day, I wasn't seeing measurable growth or promotion. Nothing new was happening.

All the while it seemed as if everyone else was moving on to the next exciting chapters of their lives. On social media, the people I followed were experiencing breakthrough. In just a simple scroll, I saw that one friend had gotten engaged—the same friend I remember praying with that we would both meet our husbands someday. Only her prayer got answered.

Another person announced her podcast had hit the top one hundred in popularity. And she'd started hers three years later than I had.

Another announced she was pregnant with her first baby. And here I was, not even dating anyone for the past six years.

While I was in waiting, it seemed as if everyone else was in progress. I couldn't help but compare my season of sowing with their season of harvest.

I so desired to see breakthrough in my relationships, my business, my calling, even my life as a whole—but it just kept feeling like I was waking up to the same day. I had no idea when my harvest would come. Despite all the time I spent in prayer, I felt so unseen and forgotten by God. I was discouraged that I couldn't see any fruit resulting from the effort I put in, day in and day out.

I had to remind myself that I wasn't the only one who ever felt that way.

In fact, you, my friend, might find yourself in a similar situation today.

Maybe you relate to this season of life not measuring up to your expectations. Maybe you are struggling to see the fruit of your labor. Maybe it feels like you keep praying the same prayers and God isn't moving on any of them. You wonder if the effort you put in on any given day makes any difference at all. And if you were to admit it, you'd say that some days you really just want to quit.

Don't Waste the Waiting

I remember one particular night that felt unusually dark and long. I sobbed to the Lord, wondering why I wasn't experiencing any significant change in my life or any crazy breakthrough. (I should tell you that I'm one of those people who rarely cry, but when I do, it's not a pretty sight.) Through my tears, I laid all my fears and my sorrows at His feet. I was honest with Him. Here I was, waking up to what seemed like the same day, being faithful in the same things . . . and I could see nothing changing. I felt like God had forgotten me.

And in that moment, a verse came into my heart: "Let us not become weary in doing good, for at the proper time we will reap a harvest if we do not give up" (Galatians 6:9). God was reassuring me that no matter how many days look the same, eventually there *has* to be fruit from faithfulness. There will be a harvest from all the seeds I've faithfully sown. And that's the unshakable reminder I needed.

The same promise is true for you.

There is a season for planting seeds that God told you to plant, and there is a season for reaping the benefits of all that you sowed in the ground. But what is hard to remember is that after you plant a seed and water it, it doesn't immediately sprout. It takes *time* for that plant to grow. It takes patience to see the fruit of your labor.

As I look back now on this season of little change, I realize God had a plan all along—one where the first step of the process led to the next, which led to the next, which led to the next. At that time, I was focused on building a team, which led me to be more consistent with content creation. One piece of content was a morning routine video, which my now-best friend, Ally Yost, stumbled across on social media. Meeting Ally eventually led me to the next season of my life, when I moved across the country to Los Angeles. So, if I hadn't built the team, I wouldn't have had the capacity to create as much and I wouldn't have been connected to one of the most important people in my life.

The process all started by staying faithful to what God called me to do, day after day, even though I wasn't seeing results.

If you feel like you keep waking up to the same day, over and over again, you are not alone. But the sowing season always comes before the harvest season. God promises us that no matter how stagnant things may seem, there will always be fruit to our labor. Hear me clearly: Just because you can't see any growth doesn't mean that nothing is going on beneath the surface. And if your situation feels completely out of control, God still encourages you to be faithful with what He's given you.

As we navigate through *The Sowing Season,* I'll share my experiences to help you make the most of your current season and keep planting good seeds where God has placed you, even if it feels insignificant right now. Together, we'll discover how to become godly women, the women we were created to be. As a result, we'll see that true success is less about future outcomes and more about being steadfast in our current circumstances.

The world refers to this steadfastness as "habits." However, God doesn't mention habits in the Bible. Instead, He emphasizes the importance of *faithfulness.* And faithfulness is often the key to unlock the next exciting season of our lives.

Today you might feel completely stuck, as if there is nothing you really can do. But God gives you more only when you make the most of what you already have. He just might be showing you that the way to progress to the next season of your life is to steward well what He's given you today. Just because you don't see your situation changing doesn't mean you need to sit still.

I want you to win. I want you to see breakthrough in each area of your life. I want you to reap a harvest in your friendships, in your relationship with God, in your health, in your calling and purpose. As we work together in this book, we're committing to not give up—no matter how many days feel the same or how far away our harvest seems.

There is much sowing to be done when we're waiting on God. But we can be sure the harvest is coming.

The Sowing Season

1

Breaking Free from Lukewarm Living

BEING FAITHFUL IN YOUR RELATIONSHIP WITH GOD

If someone were to view my daily routine with God on social media, they might think my relationship with God was always like this. But they would be surprised to know that, for a long time, I didn't center my life on God at all.

I didn't read my Bible every day. I thought it was quite boring and intimidating.

I didn't wake up early. I slept through most of my alarms and rushed through my morning.

I didn't talk to God much. In fact, I didn't even really know who He was.

I would try to resist temptation and living in worldly ways—but after trying, I would just find myself falling back into old sin cycles. (I'll be talking more about those in the pages to come.) As a result, I would feel bad about myself and question my relationship with God again.

If you know me now, you might be thinking, *Really, Ash-*

ley? I don't believe it. Give me more details. So, let me share what a typical week looked like for me several years ago:

> It's a Monday morning. I'm eighteen years old, a sophomore in college. When I wake, my head is aching, the classic symptom of having too much to drink at a party the night before.
>
> Looking at my phone on my bedside table, I notice it's only 7:30 A.M. *Surely I can sleep in until the very last minute before I have to go to my 8:30 class. And surely I don't need to set another alarm, because my body won't fall into a deep enough sleep for me to miss my class. And this bed is just so comfortable . . .*
>
> I wake up. It feels weird, like something is wrong. My headache is still there, and I need to take a shower. *What time is it?* My phone shows 8:20. *Shoot. Class starts in ten minutes.*
>
> I hop out of bed as quickly as I can, throw on a sweater and jeans, and apply the quickest makeup routine of my life. I then run to class, arriving ten minutes late. Everyone stares at me as I find my seat. *How embarrassing.*
>
> On Sunday morning I will follow this pattern all over again. Except instead of being late to school, this time I will barely make it on time for church. And I'll try my absolute hardest to scrub off the hand stamp from the bar before I enter the sanctuary. Change, at this point in my life, feels like a million miles away.

It took a lot for me to change my "morning routine," but I finally did. And if you want to have a healthy relationship with God, you have the power to change whatever you need to in order to begin growing closer to Him. Maybe you want to know how to leave the worldly lifestyle behind without having a single desire to go back. Maybe you're not sure how to be a light to your friends or how to discern who in your life is holding you back from changing and growing closer to God.

You might be struggling today to overcome being a lukewarm Christian. The Bible talks about living a lukewarm life in Revelation 3:15–16: "I know your works, that you are neither cold nor hot. I could wish you were cold or hot. So then, because you are lukewarm, and neither cold nor hot, I will vomit you out of My mouth" (NKJV). If you're not sure what it means to be lukewarm, it's being neither hot nor cold about faith in Jesus—wanting a little bit of what the world offers and a little bit of what Jesus offers. When it comes to faith, a lukewarm person isn't particularly stoked about it. Maybe they go through the motions of attending church and reading their Bible, but they aren't all in. Maybe they desire the good gifts God promises but still want to fit in with the world.

If you relate to this description, I'm glad you're here. I hold no judgment, because that was my story too. You are not alone or too far gone. I know I needed to hear this when I was in my lukewarm phase. I also know that becoming a godly woman would have taken a lot less time and would have been a whole lot easier if I had a big sister to show me how.

I'd like to be that sister to you and journey with you, friend, if you'll let me. Because you picked up this book, it means you also signed up for some change. In this chapter, I'll share with you the events that led to me recommitting my life to God. We'll discuss how to have intimacy with Him and commit your whole life to Him. And I'll include tips on how to be disciplined in your everyday routine by waking up early and getting into your Bible first thing in the morning. It starts with a desire for connection.

Recommit to God

I couldn't expect to receive much from God if I wasn't giving my whole self to Him.

I wanted to be on fire for Him. I wanted to feel close to Him. I wanted to feel joy and peace. But it was no wonder that God felt so far away when I wasn't making it my number one priority to be close to Him.

It makes me think of Matthew 16:24–26: "Jesus said to his disciples, 'Whoever wants to be my disciple must deny themselves and take up their cross and follow me. For whoever wants to save their life will lose it, but whoever loses their life for me will find it. What good will it be for someone to gain the whole world, yet forfeit their soul? Or what can anyone give in exchange for their soul?' "

Jesus gave us everything. He died on the cross for us so we would be able to have direct access to God the Father. If He made the ultimate sacrifice of laying down His whole life for us, doesn't it make sense that we would do the same for Him?

I had to come to terms with the fact that I wouldn't be close to God if I was also clinging to things of this world. If

I was still getting drunk on Saturday nights. If I was still in relationships I shouldn't be in, doing things I shouldn't be doing. If I wanted to be cool to fit in with my sorority sisters . . . but also go to Bible study. Being lukewarm didn't feel right to me, because it wasn't ever in God's best plan for my life.

I wasn't feeling close to God, because I wasn't pleasing Him with the way I was living. And by making these life choices, I was grieving the Holy Spirit.

But the Lord was gracious and merciful toward me. He started to chase me down, and I finally found my way back to Him.

When He knocks on the door of your heart again and again, it's hard to ignore forever. In case you don't know my testimony, I want to share about how I went from living lukewarm to being on fire for God.

My Very Messy Story

It was my junior year of college. I was having the typical college experience, complete with living in a sorority, drinking on the weekends, and fooling around with my boyfriend. Sure, I'd go to church—but I was also partaking in things of the world.

Right around November, my boyfriend of four years and I decided to split. It was a mutual decision, but when you've dated someone for that long, it's difficult to move on and immediately go back to normal life.

One day, about a month later, when I was home for winter break, my dad took me to Barnes & Noble. It was one of our favorite things to do together. I would go immediately to the Christian book section, and he would go to the history section. Then we would sit in silence in the bookstore café, slices of cheesecake in front of us, and flip through our books.

This bookstore excursion started like any other, but as we were driving home, my dad looked over at me and said, "Ashley, I have to tell you something. I know it's going to be very difficult to hear."

When someone tells you that, you brace yourself for what's coming next, because you know it's not going to be good.

His tone became even more serious. "Your mother and I are getting a divorce."

The moments after that are sort of a blur, but I remember being in total shock. All I could do was repeat "What? . . . *What?*"

After that conversation, things would never be the same again for me. When I got home, the knowledge of my mom and dad's divorce clouded my formerly joyful childhood home. A few days later, I watched as my dad moved his things out of our house.

That's when I began to question God.

Why would a good, loving Father allow two such horrible things to happen to me back to back? Couldn't He have been a little kinder to space out my breakup with my boyfriend and the breakup of my parents?

It was like my world was crashing down.

I would love to tell you, dear friend, that I ran to God. That I began to read my Bible more. Maybe even that I prayed about the confused feelings I was having about my faith.

But no, I did the exact opposite. I returned to school and turned away from God. I went from lukewarm to completely cold.

Within the first week back, I was drinking excessively and running to the party scene to fill the void in my crumbling life. I wanted to numb my pain with the dim lights of the bar and the attention I got from guys who really didn't care about me at all.

I did this for about a year, repeating the same cycle again and again. It never felt fulfilling, but it numbed me enough to keep me coming back for more. I kept returning to the same things that always left me feeling empty, just as Proverbs 26:11 says: "As a dog returns to its vomit, so fools repeat their folly."

Sometimes the Lord will allow you to feel the pain of your sin so you realize the destruction you're walking in. I know this to be true, as one particular evening I was shaken by the reality of my sin.

It was a cold November night in Ohio. I was with a guy at a party, and we went back to his room. And after a long night of drinking, all I wanted to do was go to sleep.

But he didn't want to go to bed just yet. I told him that I wasn't interested in doing anything sexual. And that's when he kicked me out of his room, at 2:00 A.M. He refused to let me stay until morning, because I didn't sleep with him.

Wearing nothing but a mini dress, I stood alone in the winter night. With no one around me—no one to protect me—I walked home, crying.

Thoughts of shame swirled through my now-sober mind. *How did I get here? How did everything become so hopeless? How did I become someone I don't even recognize anymore?*

A few weeks later, I went home for winter break. Here I was—a year after the news of my parents' divorce—back at home where it all began.

The next day, I woke up in my childhood bedroom, with all the lights off and the shades drawn. As I lay there, I felt completely depressed, not even able to get out of bed. I looked at myself, filled with so much shame. Everything I had done, the people I had hurt, the person I had become . . . it all made me feel so hopeless and desperate for change.

The world of escape I had turned to didn't offer the healing and purpose I had thought it would bring me. I was sick and tired of being sick and tired.

I was at a point where getting drunk wasn't even fun anymore, and the hangovers surely did get old. This lifestyle only left me hollow. Seeking validation from guys made me feel even more alone than before. I felt so empty.

It had been more than a year since I had truly gone to God for help. Lying there that morning, in my mess, in the pit of my sin and shame, I sensed I wasn't alone in my room. A polite Presence seemed to be with me, one that was certainly not going to barge in. One that wasn't going to force me to do anything or say much at all. But one that was there, right in the middle of my sorrow and pain, and wasn't scared of it one bit.

I felt this Presence then reach out its hand to me, to pull me out of the pit I was in.

And I felt this voice say, so very gently. "Ash, I want you to heal. But I want you to heal with Me."

I realized I didn't have to go back to the way I was living. I didn't have to keep the same habits that always left me feeling empty. And I could start again, here, with my heavenly Father. The life God would offer me had to be better than the hell I was living in. But I knew I wouldn't experience all that God had to offer me if I wasn't offering all of myself to Him.

It was that moment that I recommitted my life to Jesus.

So, what happened then? I returned to college a few weeks later with a renewed desire to change my way of living. I stopped drinking. I cut off those relationships with the boys who didn't respect me. I threw away my old lifestyle. Things were amazing.

And then in March, coronavirus hit. I went home as a senior in college, unsure what to do next. But my Bible was there, collecting dust on a shelf. And I actually had time to read it now.

For the next few months, I dove headfirst into the Word of God. I had so much fun with Jesus, soaking in like a sponge everything I was learning. Even though I was living in my childhood bedroom, with not a clue of what I would do next with my life, I was happy.

I danced and worshipped in my room, just me and Jesus.

I prayed and practiced hearing the voice of God.

I dreamed and took steps of faith in what I felt He was calling me to do.

And ever since I tasted and saw that life with Jesus is so much sweeter, I haven't looked back.

It's Time to Commit to Jesus

Maybe today you find yourself in a situation like mine. Maybe you're sick and tired of going back to your sin. Going back to people to find your worth. Going back to the parties. Going back to the things that make you feel terrible. You're done with feeling this way and feeling far from God.

Or maybe you've never started a relationship with God before, and you're ready to take the leap—to trust Him with your whole life.

I'm inviting you, friend, on a journey of following God and committing your whole being to Him.

Right now, we have the opportunity to commit—or recommit—to following Jesus. With all our hearts. We're going to go all in with Him and never look back.

So if you're in, say this prayer with me:

> Dear Jesus, thank You for giving me another chance. I admit that I'm a sinner and I need a Savior. I don't want to go back to the sin that brings destruction to my life. I trust that You died and rose again to pay for my sin. And I accept You, Jesus, as Lord and Savior of my life. In Your precious name, I pray. Amen.

No Turning Back

It's time we repent and turn toward Jesus.

The word *repent* used to scare me, and I think it's because

I didn't fully understand what it meant. But repentance is really quite simple. It's where you basically say, "God, I see that *Your* way is so much better than *my* way." And you turn away from the path you've been going down to follow Jesus and *His* path for you.

I had to realize that if I truly wanted to thrive with Jesus, the way I was doing things wasn't going to cut it anymore. I needed to turn away from my old ways (repent) and turn toward God.

You might be thinking . . .

Ashley, you don't know what I did yesterday. Or even a few hours ago.

And guess what? I don't care.

And Jesus doesn't either.

He just cares about a heart that is willing to follow Him. Lamentations 3:22–23 says, "The steadfast love of the LORD never ceases; his mercies never come to an end; they are new every morning; great is your faithfulness" (ESV). And 2 Corinthians 5:17 says, "If anyone is in Christ, the new creation has come: The old has gone, the new is here!"

So if you're ready to walk in freedom, now is the time for you to turn away from the sin you've been living in and turn back to God. I promise you, He will welcome you with open arms. He's already been waiting for you to go all in with Him.

Just like He did for me.

Build Your Relationship with God 101

So how do you fall in love with someone?

You get to know them.

And how do you get to know someone?

You spend time with them.

I think of the many crushes I've had. With each one, I felt an overwhelming desire to be around that person 24/7. My infatuation made me want to never leave their side, and I was willing to do almost anything to be with them.

To avoid being lukewarm, we must commit to being with Jesus every single day. Just as in a marriage, where a good relationship requires daily presence and effort, your relationship with Jesus also needs daily attention.

I had to realize that God isn't just someone I make time for on Sundays or at my weekly Bible study. He is my entire life and wants to be in every aspect of it.

So, let's get started on how you, too, can spend time with God in your everyday.

My Morning Routine with Jesus

My mornings with Jesus are sacred. For the past five years, I don't think I've missed a single day. Sometimes it looks like spending an hour with Him, while other days it might be only five minutes. I believe God is pleased with both. I'll go into more detail about how to study the Bible and read it every day in chapter 2, but for now, I'll give you an abbreviated version.

My daily routine starts with waking up around six o'clock and heading to the kitchen for a glass of water. After that, I make a cup of coffee or matcha.

Once I grab my hot drink, Bible, and journal, I head to a

comfortable chair in the living room. My favorite mornings are when it's still dark out and no one else is awake. It's just me and Him spending time with each other. Some days I ask God what I should read, then flip to the first scripture I feel He says. Other times I look up the daily reading in my Bible app or choose a book of the Bible to explore. But before I begin digging in, I ask the Holy Spirit to speak to me as I spend time in His Word. I sit with God and talk to Him and journal.

After my morning time with God, I take Him with me throughout my day. I take Him into the mundane, everyday things I'm doing: exercising, eating, working, being with friends, and sleeping.

I noticed that as I draw near to God and focus on being close to Him throughout the day, He actually *feels* closer. Jeremiah 29:13 has a promise for us: "You will seek me and find me when you seek me with all your heart."

When you make it your aim to seek Him with your entire heart, you will find Him. You will get to know Him. And not only that; you also will fall in love with Him. And it won't be you living vicariously through me—it will be your own unique relationship with God.

Once you get to truly know Him and His love for you, you won't turn back to any lesser pleasure that this world offers. Because His love is just that good.

About Those Early Mornings . . .

You don't have to wake up early to spend time with God. After all, maybe you have a schedule where this simply isn't possible. But if you don't have any legitimate excuses, let me encourage you that spending time with God in the early hours of the morning—just you and Him and a good cup of coffee—is one of the most peaceful things you can do. It will set the tone for the rest of your day.

But what if you're just not a morning person? I get it—I didn't used to be one either.

As I told you previously, I was the person who would wake up at the very last minute, rush out of bed, and have the most chaotic start to the day. I was certainly *not* a morning person, which might be a surprise to some. But over the years, the Lord has helped me not only consistently wake up early but also become someone who looks forward to having an early-morning routine with God.

These are some things that have helped me wake up early:

1. **Go to bed early the night before.** This is *so* important. I used to go to bed at midnight and then wonder why it was so difficult to wake up at five the next morning. When I got into a habit of going to sleep early, it became much easier to wake up early. This meant being diligent about putting my phone away an hour before I had to fall asleep. I also can get to sleep easier if I take magnesium thirty minutes to an hour before bed. In my ideal routine, I fall asleep at ten, then wake up around five or six.
2. **Keep the alarm out of arm's reach.** Before going to bed, I set my phone alarm but put my phone across the room. This prevents me from shutting off my alarm in the morning, accidentally or on purpose, by simply reaching over to turn it off. By putting my phone across the room, I

have to get up to turn it off, which helps me not press snooze.

3. **Create an enjoyable morning routine.** If I know my delicious matcha latte and spending time in the presence of God are on the other side of waking up early, it definitely helps me get out of bed. My morning routine might not look the same as yours, but it's important you create a routine that will make you want to get out of bed.

How to Spend Time with God Every Day

Now that we've conquered the chore of waking up early, perhaps you want to know how to actually spend time with God. Here are a few things I've learned over the years about how to spend intimate time with my heavenly Father:

1. **Decide on a time you will spend together every day.** As we talked about before, maybe morning won't work for you if you have weird work hours or school or if it's just too difficult to find a time in the morning to get alone with God. That's okay. For you, it could be on the bus on the way to school, or at lunchtime when your kids are at school, or in the evening when life has settled down. Whatever your schedule is, pre-decide on a time every day when you are going to make spending time with God a priority. It's kind of like working out—if you don't decide to do it every day at a certain time, you likely won't keep it up, because it's not always fun going to the gym and moving your body.

2. **Include Him in everything you do.** God doesn't want to be in parts of your day. He wants to have all your day and to be a part of every single thing you do. You get to include the Lord in the mundane things and the exciting things of your everyday life. I make a conscious effort to think of Him and include Him in my activities, as if He were right next to me the entire time.
3. **Pray about everything.** In Scripture, we see that we are supposed to "pray without ceasing" (1 Thessalonians 5:17, ESV). We can absolutely talk to God in everything we do. I talk to God in the shower, during my workouts, when I'm on a walk, when I'm cooking, when I'm in the grocery store, and more. And as soon as I get a fearful or anxious thought, I lift it up to Him in prayer. When I need guidance or wisdom, I'm quick to ask for counsel from the Holy Spirit. Building a habit of talking to God all the time will help reassure you that He's with you all the time (because He is).
4. **Spend time in godly community.** Spending time with friends who love Jesus can also be sweet time between you and your Savior. He tells us that "where two or three gather in my name, there am I with them" (Matthew 18:20). You and your friends can do Bible study together, pray together, worship the Lord together. You don't have to follow Him on your own. (Don't have Christian friends? More on this in chapter 4.)
5. **Listen to worship music.** When I'm working out, driving, cooking, or even working, that is a great time for me to listen to worship music. You're welcome to access the many playlists I've created on Spotify (@ashleymorganh).

It's just a simple way to include God in your everyday life, even with a busy schedule. And you can worship Him while you're doing the most mundane task.

6. **Ask for accountability.** Despite trying to make God your number one priority, you will have days when you want to fall back into your old ways—when being faithful is the last thing you want to do. This is when there's nothing sweeter than having a friend who can hold you accountable, pray for you, and help you in your walk with God. Ask this friend to check in on you about your Bible reading plan or your prayer life. Or you could even make it a goal to listen to worship music instead of secular music at the gym. Having accountability will help you grow closer to God and become who He created you to be.

As we go on this journey through this book together, know that it takes baby steps to eventually make huge strides with God. And just know that you are not alone. I'll be holding your hand the whole way there.

I believe you can grow closer to God than you ever have.

I believe He'll transform you into a completely different person. Because that's what He loves to do. If He can do it in my life, He can surely do it in yours.

2

Letting the Word of God Transform You

BEING FAITHFUL IN READING THE BIBLE

I didn't grow up in a home where my parents read nightly Bible stories to me. My view of the Bible at that time was shaped by culture, which portrayed it as boring and outdated.

Right after getting saved, I did the typical Christian thing of going to Barnes & Noble and buying the cutest Bible I could find. But since I didn't know how to actually read it, my Bible sat on my desk for years, looking cute but completely untouched.

Meanwhile, I wondered why I couldn't let go of my lukewarm lifestyle. Why I couldn't stop partying. Why I kept slipping up, time and time again. I didn't believe that the Bible could provide direction for my life or answer any questions I had—or that I'd even be able to understand it all if it did.

But when I decided in college to turn away from the sinful life I was living and go all in with God, I knew that reading the Bible was something I would have to discipline myself to do.

I thought back to a meeting I had during high school with my Young Life leader, before I really went all in with Jesus. We both loved books. So I asked her what her favorite book was, and with eyes wide, she grabbed her Bible and said, "This." I rolled my eyes. *How could this outdated book from thousands of years ago even apply to me today?* Thinking about this years later, I realized she had read a lot of books and the fact that she could point to this one as her favorite was certainly saying something. *What am I missing?* I wondered. *Maybe it's time to try to read it for myself.*

When I started reading the Bible, I was intimidated by it. It took many years and much trial and error to finally get to a place where I would read the Bible every day. I had to learn tips for getting started and how to read it when I didn't feel like it.

Maybe you're in a similar position now—where you want to read the Bible but struggle to read it every day. Maybe you don't know where to start or how long to read. And you might not know how this ancient book can apply to your life today or help you have a strong relationship with God.

In this chapter, we're covering everything you need to know to read the Bible daily so that you can genuinely love reading it, grow closer to God, and reach your full potential in Him.

But before we get into the how behind reading the Bible—let's get into why it's good for us to read this book consistently.

Reading the Bible Is Good for You

Here's the truth: The Bible isn't one long, outdated book from thousands of years ago. It's a collection of historical documents that were compiled into one big book. It was written by about forty authors over the course of 1,500 years, and it's all God's story of bringing redemption to humanity. Each story is equally relevant to us today.

The Bible is God's Word, God's truth. He chose to speak through these different authors through His Spirit. As God's Word, the Bible is the primary way God speaks to us.

Early on, I struggled to believe that God spoke through every single writer in the Bible. I easily accepted the idea that Jesus's words, highlighted in red in the Scriptures, were God's words. I believed that Jesus's teachings were the most crucial to focus on but that Paul's writings were less significant—partly because I didn't like everything Paul said. But 2 Timothy 3:16–17 says, "All Scripture is God-breathed and is useful for teaching, rebuking, correcting and training in righteousness, so that the servant of God may be thoroughly equipped for every good work." This meant I had to let go of my pride and believe that *every* verse was from God, even the ones I didn't like, and it wasn't my place to determine what God's truth is. This is just another example of what I had to fully surrender—dictating what is and isn't important in the Bible.

If you're like me and need more than one reason to get behind something, here are several more reasons it's good for you to read the Word daily:

- to grow closer to God (1 Peter 2:2)
- to know God's will and have direction for your life (Psalm 119:105)
- to have strength, comfort, and hope (Psalm 119:50)
- to have joy (Psalm 16:11)
- to discern good from evil (Psalm 119:101)
- to be changed from the inside out (Romans 12:2)
- to understand God's love for you (John 4:16)
- to get rid of anxiety and have peace (Psalm 119:165)

Consistently reading my Bible led to a huge transformation in me, from the party girl who was lukewarm in all her ways to the girl who was so in love with Jesus that He was all she could talk about. After I spent months diving into my Bible in my post-grad years, other people noticed the change in me as well—some even asking, "What happened to you?"

Intimacy with God played a huge role in transforming me from the inside out, but so did reading the Bible every day and letting the Word of God shape the way I see myself and the world.

I love what Romans 12:2 says: "Do not conform to the pattern of this world, but be transformed by the renewing of your mind. Then you will be able to test and approve what God's will is—his good, pleasing and perfect will." In other words, if we want to be godly women and truly walk as Jesus walked, we must begin by transforming our minds. This transformation involves our thoughts and the influences we permit to shape them. A significant way we can change our thoughts—and our lives—is by daily Bible reading, allowing the Word of God to transform our very being.

Tips for Consistent Bible Reading

Let's be honest. You are not always going to feel like doing something that's good for you. In fact, the things that are best for us are rarely things we will *want* to do.

Whether it's choosing to drink a glass of water instead of a Coke, choosing to eat a salad instead of a doughnut, or choosing to go for a run instead of sleeping in, we as humans don't find that discipline comes naturally.

But discipline gets easier the more you flex that muscle.

The way you get fit is to go to the gym and eat healthy, which isn't always fun. But the way you build this lifestyle of working out and eating healthy is by committing to it, even if you don't want to. That's how you see results.

The same is true of Bible reading. Just because some days you don't feel like reading your Bible doesn't mean you shouldn't read it. It just means you must discipline yourself to do the things you don't always feel like doing.

And as you discipline yourself every day to wake up early and get into your Bible, with a cozy drink, in a cute corner of your house, maybe you'll even look forward to your daily time with God. And that daily discipline of reading your Bible will become something you'll never want to miss.

So let's dig deeper into how to read the Bible consistently.

1. Have the Right Tools

In order to read the Bible every day, you're going to need a Bible. We're starting simple here.

When I got started with my Bible reading journey, I didn't want just any Bible. I wanted one that was cute and that had ample space to write in.

James Clear, in his book, *Atomic Habits,* stresses the importance of making good habits attractive to increase the likelihood of adopting them.[1] After all, if a behavior gives off positive feelings, you're more likely to want to do it. This is why I advocate for having a cute Bible. If your Bible is cute, you're more likely to make reading it a habit. (I especially like those from Hosanna Revival.)

If you're shopping for a Bible, you'll notice that you have a choice of several translations. The Bible was originally written in Hebrew, Aramaic, and Greek and was translated into other languages. When it comes to English translations, my favorite ones are the New International Version (NIV), New Living Translation (NLT), English Standard Version (ESV), and Christian Standard Bible (CSB). I also like Bibles that have decorative margins with ample space for note-taking.

To make the most of your Bible reading experience, you should consider having a cute journal and cute pens and highlighters too (my favorites are from Mr. Pen). We are all about forming good habits here, and I think James Clear would be proud to hear we are making *all* our supplies cute.

If you don't have a Bible and you're tight on resources, you can always access the Bible on your phone through the YouVersion app, which allows you to read the scripture of the day and takes only around five minutes.

2. Decide What to Read

Out of the sixty-six books in the Bible, I would recommend starting with the gospel of John. The word *gospel* means "good news," and the four Gospels—Matthew, Mark, Luke, and John—tell the story of Jesus's life from different perspectives. These are the first four books of the New Testament.

Next I would read Matthew. Then Romans, James, and Proverbs.

These books can be super helpful to get you started on your Bible reading journey.

3. Commit to a Bible Reading Plan

Once you've read a couple of books of the Bible, you might decide you want further help to know how to keep going. One way to read through the Bible in a logical order is to use a Bible reading plan. There are plenty of plans to choose from. Some enable you to read through the whole Bible in a year. Others guide you through the Bible chronologically or topically.

I encourage you to check out the YouVersion app or my online community the Tree,[2] which gives you a daily reading plan to follow. You can read this plan on the go, while you're on a walk or just going about your day. It's also a great way to join a community of other women who can hold you accountable.

4. Decide Where and When

I love having a cozy place in my house where I read at roughly the same time every day.

Take a look at the space you have. Where can you find a restful place you can devote to consistent reading? Maybe it's a chair in the corner of your bedroom, right by the window. Maybe it's your comfortable couch in the living room. Or by your favorite candle on your kitchen island.

Speaking from experience, I wouldn't recommend reading the Bible in bed. Many times I simply didn't want to get out of bed in the morning, so I tried reading my Bible there. The only problem with this is I would close my eyes "for a minute" shortly after opening my Bible . . . only to wake up and realize my "minute" was a half hour.

This is why I set up a cute and cozy Bible reading space that isn't cozy enough for me to fall asleep.

In my old place in Nashville, I had a little Bible reading corner in my room. Now that I live in California, I have a couch that always welcomes me in the morning hours.

Whatever you do, find a place you can read your Bible every day. And make sure it feels inviting to you.

Don't just think about where to read the Bible—but also consider the time. Ask yourself if you can wake up fifteen to thirty minutes earlier and read the Bible or if you can squeeze it in during your lunch break if you can't wake up earlier. I know not everyone has a schedule that allows them to read in the morning, so maybe commit to a time in the evening.

As I've said, I prefer reading the Bible at the start of my morning, before I check my phone. Doing so can provide many benefits: It helps me set a spiritual focus for the day, aligns my thoughts and actions with God's Word, and puts my relationship with God first. I feel my whole day is viewed through the lens of Scripture when I prioritize it first thing.

Whatever time you decide, make sure it fits your schedule so it can actually become a habit. But please, don't go from zero to one hundred. Let's go back to that gym analogy. Think back to a time when you hadn't been working out for a while and then you decided that you were going to be a gym queen by moving your body for two hours a day. That lasted for maybe three days before you burned yourself out or were so sore that you had no motivation to get back into the gym.

When that happened to me, I had to realize that if I just moved my body for thirty minutes a day five days a week, that consistency would pay off over the course of months and years. I would have more energy, be healthier, and feel stronger. Not by two hours of working out every once in a while, but because of thirty minutes of movement five times a week.

Back to Bible reading . . . I know there are plenty of people who read their Bibles for three hours a day. And truly, I love that for them. That's a gift to be so obsessed with the Word that you physically struggle to get away from it. But as for me, reading the Bible has had to be a discipline that I integrate into my daily routine. I don't beat myself up for being someone who isn't able to read her Bible for three hours a day. I'm okay with being a faithful, diligent follower of Jesus by disciplining myself to read this book every single day, even if it's just for fifteen minutes. If we're going to make following Jesus a part of our everyday life, it must be sustainable, something that we can actually commit to.

You don't need to read the Bible for multiple hours a day to have a good relationship with Jesus. Faithfulness isn't about showing up in extreme ways. Faithfulness is about showing up in simple ways, every day. Reading the Bible every day—for whatever amount of time works for you—will help you have a good relationship with Jesus. As long as you're opening it up.

5. Study the Scriptures

When we study anything, it's natural for us to ask questions about it.

I remember being in my freshman-year calculus class. I kept raising my hand throughout the class because I had no idea what the professor was saying half the time. (I'm sure my classmates loved that.) But getting answers helped me make sense of the material.

When we read the Bible, it's healthy to ask questions. One of the best ways I've found to do this is to go through the SOAP Bible study method:[3]

Scripture: As you read, write down the scriptures that stand out the most to you.

Observation: What truth stood out to you? Are there any warnings, principles, or commands in the verses? What is the author saying?

Application: How can you apply these scriptures to your everyday life?

Prayer: Turn these thoughts into a prayer. Ask the Lord to help you meditate on these scriptures throughout the day and apply them to your life.

6. Consult Other Translations

After I do my Bible reading for the day, I like to go into the YouVersion app and read key verses in multiple translations. This helps me squeeze all the meaning out of the scripture I'm reading. I don't do this every day, but when I really want to get a full grasp of the text, I will go about it this way.

Bible translations I usually flip through are the New Living Translation (NLT), The Message (MSG), and the Amplified Bible, Classic Edition (AMPC).

7. Refer to a Commentary

For a long time, I didn't know what a commentary was, so I didn't think it would be very revolutionary in my time with God. But I was so wrong.

A commentary is a written explanation and interpretation of the Bible. It analyzes books of the Bible verse by verse. A commentary examines the historical context, who wrote the text, and other relevant facts about the Scriptures, allowing you to get greater insight into and meaning out of the text.

My favorite commentary is by David Guzik at Enduring Word. (Tip: Google the verse + David Guzik, and you'll find a great commentary to help you understand the scripture you're reading!)

8. Journal Your Revelations

I used to journal to myself. Now I journal to God.

As I read my commentary and answer those observation and application questions from the SOAP method, I journal my thoughts. I also write what I learn about the scripture from my commentary. Writing my thoughts down helps me remember the scripture, and it becomes part of me.

You don't have to follow a strict regimen with this—you can just journal what's on your heart that day. Consider it like a little love note to God.

Journal your thoughts, prayers, revelations. Just God and you will see it—so don't be afraid to be honest.

9. Start and End with Prayer

The quiet hours of the morning are such a sweet time to talk to God. In Mark 1:35, we see that Jesus followed this model as well: "Very early in the morning, while it was still dark, Jesus got up, left the house and went off to a solitary place, where he prayed."

If Jesus got up very early in the morning to pray, shouldn't we?

There's something so beautiful when I sit with my Bible open in my lap and bring my thoughts and revelations to God in prayer. I first ask God to speak to me through His Word and reveal to me the truth He wants to show me that day. When I started reading the Bible, I felt that I was flying through the pages, and not much was really resonating with me. Then I heard a pastor say, "You must pray before reading your Bible. Simply say, 'Holy Spirit, I ask that You would speak to me through Your Word.' "

As soon as I heard this, I started to implement it into my daily Bible reading routine. And it truly made the biggest difference. New revelations and realizations that I previously would have skipped over began to jump off the page. The

Holy Spirit was, in fact, showing me what He wanted to teach me through the holy Word of God.

Here's a good, simple prayer before reading the Bible each day:

> Father, I ask that You speak to me through Your Word today. I give You this Bible study time and ask that You reveal what You want to teach me. Help me grow closer to You. Amen.

After I'm done reading, I again turn to God in prayer. I thank Him for what He showed me in my quiet time, and I ask Him to help me apply the daily reading to my life. Then I ask Him to help me with my day.

Lifting my thoughts to God in prayer and asking Him to be with me for that day makes a world of a difference in sealing my quiet time with God.

10. Highlight or Underline Verses That Speak to You

In high school, I was taught in English class to annotate my books, meaning to make notes on or mark up a text with thoughts, questions, or realizations. I discovered that annotating helps me actually pay attention to what I'm reading.

I realized I could do the same with my Bible.

After all, when you're reading something early in the morning, it can be hard to lock in. By writing notes and highlighting what I feel the Spirit is revealing to me, I can focus better and stay awake.

11. Drink a Fun Drink

This past year, I noticed that my stress levels were high at certain points in the day, especially after drinking coffee. After much research, I found that drinking coffee in the morning isn't good for stress levels.

So with that, I decided to cut coffee out of my morning routine. But what I didn't realize was that I was also cutting out a sweet part of my time with Jesus.

See, for years, I had set a morning routine of making my coffee and then reading my Bible. It was like a sacred ritual I had with the Lord.

When I cut out my cup of coffee, reading the Bible wasn't as enjoyable for me (that's me just being real). It became much more tempting to skip my daily Bible reading.

By eliminating my coffee ritual, I was violating two techniques—habit stacking and temptation bundling—that help create a new habit. According to James Clear in *Atomic Habits*,

> **Habit stacking** is where you intentionally place a new habit right after an existing one in your routine so that you're more likely to make the new habit a part of your daily ritual. When I took my existing habit (morning coffee) out of my routine, it made it harder for me to keep doing my new habit (Bible reading).
>
> **Temptation bundling** is where you link a less desirable activity with an enjoyable one to make the former more appealing. In my case, the enjoyable activity was

> drinking my coffee. The less desirable one was reading my Bible. When I eliminated the daily coffee ritual, I was less inclined to read the Bible.[4]

It's no wonder I was struggling to read my Bible in the morning. So I made a change. I switched my daily cup of coffee to matcha, which is much less of a cortisol spike. Of course, sometimes I still enjoy a protein coffee in the morning. But just from not getting rid of this little caffeine boost, I'm locked into my Bible again.

12. Read the Bible with Other People

Reading the Bible with other people can make a big difference. Doing so provides encouragement and accountability, and we can help one another grow in knowledge and godliness when we do it together.

There are so many ways to read the Bible with other people. Maybe you have a friend you can commit to a reading plan with. Or maybe you can join a Bible study through a local church. Perhaps there is a school ministry you can get plugged into. You can always join my community I mentioned earlier—the Tree—where hundreds of other women with the same goals as you can hold you accountable through our weekly live group calls. We will welcome you with open arms!

But whatever it looks like, reading with others can help you understand the Bible and apply it to your life. I can't tell you the number of times when I've been studying Scripture with others and one of my friends noticed something different in the text than I did. This allowed me to learn so much more. It's amazing to see how the Spirit moves when we read the Word and pray with other believers. I love what Matthew 18:20 says: "Where two or three gather in my name, there am I with them."

Reading the Bible with other people lets you hear other perspectives, and it makes reading the Bible more fun.

Let God's Word Change You

So much fruit comes from disciplining yourself to get in the Word every single day.

Jesus uses a parable in Matthew 13:3–8 to teach about the power of the Word of God:

> A farmer went out to sow his seed. As he was scattering the seed, some fell along the path, and the birds came and ate it up. Some fell on rocky places, where it did not have much soil. It sprang up quickly, because the soil was shallow. But when the sun came up, the plants were scorched, and they withered because they had no root. Other seed fell among thorns, which grew up and choked the plants. Still other seed fell on good soil, where it produced a crop—a hundred, sixty or thirty times what was sown.

Jesus then interprets the meaning to the disciples:

> When anyone hears the message about the kingdom and does not understand it, the evil one comes and snatches

> away what was sown in their heart. This is the seed sown along the path. The seed falling on rocky ground refers to someone who hears the word and at once receives it with joy. But since they have no root, they last only a short time. When trouble or persecution comes because of the word, they quickly fall away. The seed falling among the thorns refers to someone who hears the word, but the worries of this life and the deceitfulness of wealth choke the word, making it unfruitful. But the seed falling on good soil refers to someone who hears the word and understands it. This is the one who produces a crop, yielding a hundred, sixty or thirty times what was sown. (verses 19–23)

The Word of God is a seed. It gets planted in our hearts and then has the potential to bear fruit.

We see in Scripture that when the Word is received as it should be, something happens in our hearts and fruit is produced.

But Satan, our enemy, doesn't want the Word of God to take root in our hearts. We see that when people start reading the Bible but then get bored and stop. Or when people are diligent in going to church but then something—a distraction, sin, or boredom—causes them to give up.

The enemy will use anything to prevent us from receiving the Word of God, because he knows the Word of God will change our lives. For me, it wasn't behavior modification that got me to stop binge drinking and being in unhealthy relationships. Despite my continuous efforts to avoid drinking excessively, I always ended up failing. What truly made the difference was reading the Bible—not only reading it, but also letting it change me. I had to get so deep in the Word that it would change my root structure and develop me into a person I couldn't even recognize anymore. When I was tempted to go get drunk or text that boy that wasn't good for me, I would hear a scripture in my mind about drunkenness or being unequally yoked with unbelievers. Slowly but surely, God was changing my mindset and thoughts, and it was bearing fruit on the outside.

The way to change into a godly woman—the person God created you to be—isn't to try harder. It's to diligently read the Word of God and let it transform the way you think. And when you change the way you think, your actions will soon follow. You will begin to not even recognize yourself.

I've become so in love with Scripture—with letting God speak to me through His Word—that it's as if the Word of God has been written on my heart. When I ask God to speak to me about something, what comes to my mind is Scripture. When a friend asks me for advice, what comes to my mind is Scripture.

And even as I write this book, most of what comes to my mind is Scripture.

The same will happen for you. When you read the Bible every day, the Word of God becomes written on your heart. Then, over the course of months and years, the Holy Spirit will build a reservoir in your mind and heart filled with God's words—something you can draw from to help you with every difficulty. When you get into the Word of God, the Word of God will get into you.

The Bible is so important to your walk with God. And once you open it and discipline yourself to get in it every single day, you will truly never be the same.

3

Building Spiritual Resilience

BEING FAITHFUL THROUGH TEMPTATION

Two years after I went all in with Jesus, I was invited to a bachelorette party in Charleston, South Carolina. Because I had abandoned my old lifestyle of drinking and partying and because it had been years since I had been in that rhythm of going to the bars every weekend, I was sure the temptation to step back into that lifestyle was long gone. After all, I had committed to following Jesus and reading the Bible every day.

As is tradition with bachelorette parties, drinking and barhopping were a large part of the agenda. My plan was to have only one drink, then sip on sparkling water for the rest of the night.

But that one drink turned into two. And then a shot. And then another shot. And then another drink at the bar . . .

And before I knew it, I was drunk.

The rest of the night was a blur, and I made some questionable decisions in my inebriated state. I woke up with the biggest hangover, and I was embarrassed when my friends later showed me videos of myself acting belligerent the night before.

I had gotten so intoxicated that I stayed at the bar with a group of people I didn't even know, and my friend had to come find me.

I felt awful. Here I was, a committed follower of Jesus who had turned away from her old life of sin—and had severely messed up. For days and weeks after that, I couldn't help but beat myself up and fall into shame. And because I didn't think God could forgive me after I betrayed Him like that, He felt more and more distant.

I couldn't believe I had fallen into sin so easily, despite willing myself not to go back.

How to Stop Sinning

Wouldn't it be crazy if, after being baptized, we never had to struggle with sin again?

I used to wonder why I still struggled with cussing even after being baptized. Or texting those boys, which never led to anything good. Or going out to the bars. Why didn't that baptism just solve all those issues?

Even though we are born again in Christ and we are a new creation, we still must go through a process of sanctification to become the people God created us to be and to be rid of the sin in our hearts that causes a wedge between us and Him.

It can be discouraging when we feel like we keep falling

into the same old sin cycles, no matter how hard we try to turn away. Allow me to share with you the things that have helped me the most to live a holy, pure life before God, in hope this helps you on your own journey of living a life that is pleasing to Him.

1. Don't Leave a Door Open

When my beloved mentor Julie is praying for people, she always finds a way to include this: "If there's any crack or back door open, we pray in Jesus's name that it shuts and the enemy does not have any foothold in your life." Ephesians 4:27 very simply says, "Do not give the devil a foothold." Unfortunately, however, sin does sometimes find a way of creeping in when we have an open door in our lives.

The reason I fell back into sin during that bachelorette trip was that I had left a small opening for drunkenness by being willing to drink one too many drinks. I had a mindset going into the trip that it wouldn't be the end of the world if I got a little tipsy.

It's crucial to decide to close any open doors—and to keep them shut. It would have been better if I had recognized I was still fresh out of that season of struggling with drinking and pre-decided not to drink at all on the trip. It's kind of like if you say you will have only one bite of the cake that's in front of you. I don't know about you, but usually I end up eating way more than one bite. I would be better off saying no to a single bite of cake to begin with.

Oftentimes, when we open the door to the devil—even if it's just a little—he can find a way to come in and take up a lot more space in our lives than we ever intended for him to.

That's the tricky thing with the devil. He doesn't run down the streets with a red flag, saying, "Look at me! I'm the devil, trying to ruin your life!" No, he is the father of lies and the master of deception (John 8:44). That means he is awfully good at his job, good at getting people to sin, and as a result he pulls people away from God and the abundant life God has for His people.

The devil can sneak in by whispering lies to you to get you to compromise just a bit. The lie that drinking a glass of wine every day surely is okay because you're not getting drunk . . .

The lie that "doing stuff" with your boyfriend is okay because at least you're not having sex . . .

The lie that watching that TV show or listening to that music is okay because it's what everyone else watches and listens to—and it's literally trending on TikTok . . .

All these little lies aren't *that* big of a deal. Until you find yourself in a place you never thought you would be.

And you are struggling to get through the day without alcohol.

And you slipped up and had sex with your boyfriend.

And you fell back into hanging out with that old group of friends you swore you would create distance from.

And if you're like me, you found yourself with a huge hangover during one of your best friends' bachelorette weekends, feeling like a total idiot because of the night before.

The key to resisting all this damage and destruction is to not open the door to the enemy in the first place.

2. Ask God for the Strength to Resist

I've already told you what one of my biggest temptations was—I *always* used to sleep in.

All throughout high school, I would wake up to my parents knocking loudly on my door, reminding me that I had only fifteen minutes until the bus would come.

And this didn't get any better when I got to college. I would wake up at the start of my class time in the morning, frantically hop out of bed, and end up walking into class twenty minutes late, with all eyes on me. Whatever I did, I couldn't shake this bad habit of sleeping in. And I really didn't know what to do about it.

When I decided in my post–lukewarm era that I was going to be a girl who woke up early to read her Bible and then get a good workout in after—I knew I had to shake this bad habit of sleeping in until the very last minute.

I needed the reminder from 1 Corinthians 10:13:

> No temptation has overtaken you except what is common to mankind. And God is faithful; he will not let you be tempted beyond what you can bear. But when you are tempted, he will also provide a way out so that you can endure it.

After reading this scripture, I knew God would always help me find a way out of any temptation I struggled with.

When I woke up on that first alarm, I had to cry out to God and ask Him to give me the strength to get out of bed. I had to call on His name in the morning hours and ask for His help.

Over time, His Spirit led me to start going to bed earlier and putting the Francine Rivers book down when it was time to go to sleep. And asking for His strength in this area of my life really helped as well.

Now I'm a total morning person. I prefer waking up early and getting my day started when it feels like the whole world is still asleep. Only God can transform a girl who rushed through her mornings into someone who can't wait to wake up at the crack of dawn to spend time with Him.

Sleeping in is one temptation, but many of us struggle with other things.

I remember a conversation I had with a former mentor. She told me that when she and her boyfriend were together, sometimes they would feel tempted to do *more* than kiss. She said that every time things would get heated, she noticed God always provided a way out of the temptation—like a roommate would come home early, or a distraction would come up, or a knot would even develop in her stomach. Whenever she asked God to help her escape temptation, He would come through and help her and her boyfriend when they were struggling.

God has a beautiful way of giving us the strength that we need and providing a way out of temptation when it comes close.

3. Set Yourself Up for Success

It's interesting how we can pray for God's strength yet still put ourselves in situations where we know we are prone to slip up.

We might ask God to help us avoid falling into sin with

our boyfriend, but then we choose to watch movies with him late into the night, knowing that is a perfect scenario for temptation.

We might ask God to help us wake up early, but then instead of going to bed at a reasonable hour, we choose to stay up and scroll on TikTok until 1:00 A.M.

We might ask God to help us stop getting drunk, but then we choose to spend time on the weekends at the bars.

All the while, we get so upset at ourselves for slipping up.

Yes, God will provide a way out of temptation, but He wants us to use wisdom. We can do things to set ourselves up for success so we don't fall into sin in the first place.

If you are someone who struggles with emotional eating—maybe you run to the pantry and snack on chocolate and cookies and candy whenever an unpleasant feeling arises—it's probably not a good thing to have those items in your pantry at all.

In your current struggles with sin, ask God to help you create a path for success in those areas. You might have to get rid of the junk food in your cabinet, choose a different friend group for weekend activities, or commit to not being with your boyfriend past 9:00 P.M.

Setting yourself up for success in your sin-prone areas is going to help you resist temptation. Out of sight helps make it out of mind.

4. Don't Diminish the Power of Accountability

It's very difficult to withstand temptation by ourselves. And this is exactly why we need people to hold us accountable.

A few months ago, I was struggling with the way I viewed food and exercise. Unfortunately, I was making it more than a healthy lifestyle, and it was becoming something that all my life and thoughts revolved around. Slowly but surely, what started out as a passion became an idol. And I was obsessed with the way I looked and the food I consumed.

I had to take a moment to be vulnerable, and feeling led by the Holy Spirit, I asked my friend Ally to pray for me. I asked her to pray that the Lord would heal my relationship with food and exercise. And that He would help me live a healthy lifestyle while still putting Him on the throne of my heart.

And not only did I confess and ask for prayer, but I also asked for accountability moving forward. I asked Ally to check on me if she ever thought I was over-exercising, like the times when I would go to the gym for three hours a day. And I asked her to help me enjoy fun foods in my diet again, instead of always restricting myself.

The power of accountability in the weeks and months after that was huge. It was hard for me to hide anything from her, because she was also my housemate. Living in community makes it difficult to live in sin, which is why it's good not to be alone.

James 5:16 says, "Confess your sins to each other and pray for each other so that you may be healed. The prayer of a righteous person is powerful and effective." Yes, God wants you to confess your sins to Him. But He also wants you to confess your sins to other people.

Something powerful happens when you take that thing you've been struggling with, that sin you just can't shake, and you humble yourself and tell someone you can trust. What's important is not just that you are vulnerable with them but that after you confess, you also pray with the person you confessed to. Only then will there be healing.

So, to get rid of sin in our lives, we must bring those dark spaces to light. We must be willing to be vulnerable and open with those we love. We must be willing to receive prayer that God would create a change in our lives. And we must be willing to choose to go another way—to follow God's way and God's Word.

If you don't have a friend you can confess to, I encourage you to seek out any of the other resources we've mentioned: a Bible study, church community, online community (like the Tree), or school ministry.

5. Watch What You Consume

It's easier to live a life that honors God when you are consuming things that honor God.

It might be a surprise to you that I used to listen to the most vulgar music. But because it was culturally popular and usually had a catchy tune, I didn't think twice about adding it to my playlists. I even remember getting back from a Young Life camp in high school and immediately jamming out to the new Gucci Mane song as I unpacked my stuff. Christian music just wasn't my taste.

I listened to this music filled with profanity without realizing that it was affecting me in ways I couldn't see. I would find myself waking up with the most offensive lyrics stuck in my head. Because the music was catchy, it was replaying in my mind, rent-free.

I obviously didn't want these lyrics in my mind, shaping my thoughts and eventually my actions. I had to make the decision to change my music habits. I would have to see if possibly *some* Christian music might not be as bad as I had assumed.

Sure, there are some Christian songs that aren't my taste or might even feel a little outdated. But it was such a beautiful thing when the Holy Spirit led me to Christian music that matched the style of music I listened to before coming to Christ but had lyrics that were glorifying to God.

I'm convinced angels come in the room when you listen and sing to a worship song. Just the other day, I was driving in L.A. traffic, and it was really taking way longer than I thought to get to my Pilates class. Seeing all the cars and chaos surrounding me, I decided to turn on worship music and make good use of my driving time.

As I sang the worship song with all my heart, I felt the Spirit of God in the car. His peace was all over my car, His presence thick in the air, even midmorning on a Tuesday in L.A. traffic.

We can choose to listen to whatever music we want to. But if one of those music options could help me experience the literal living God, why would I deprive myself of that experience?

I know there are many enjoyable mainstream songs, ones that have nothing to do with Jesus. And they might even make us feel good. But there is so much power in putting songs in our ears that also usher in the presence of God.

I'm happy to share my Spotify playlists with you. Whether you need a playlist for the gym, getting work done at a coffee shop, or a long drive—I've got you covered with good, "vibey" Christian songs you can listen to. You can find my Spotify at @ashleymorganh.

In addition to music, we must be intentional with other media we consume. I had to let go of the TV shows and movies that didn't help me grow in my walk with Jesus and had to decide to fast-forward through scenes that might open doors to the enemy.

First Corinthians 6:12 says, " 'I have the right to do anything,' you say—but not everything is beneficial. 'I have the right to do anything'—but I will not be mastered by anything." Yes, we can listen to any type of music. And if we are of age, we can watch anything we want. But just because we can do something, does that make it beneficial for our walk with God and for living out His purpose for us?

It's important we look at the media we consume and consider if it's really helping us draw nearer to God or if it's taking us further away.

6. Choose Your Friends Wisely

One of the most significant obstacles to your relationship with God can be the company you keep.

There have been plenty of times I tried to make my faith a personal matter, meaning I kept it to myself like it was my own thing and I wasn't surrounding myself with other people of faith. In fact, the people around me were the furthest from God. I found I couldn't be close to God in these seasons when the people around me kept pulling me away.

Then a mentor gave me an analogy that completely

changed the way I see living in community: Imagine you are standing on a chair. You extend your hand to a friend and try to pull her up to stand with you on the chair. It's not easy to bring that friend up to your level. Now consider if that friend was instead trying to get you to be on the ground with her. It's much easier for her to pull you down to her level than for you to lift her up to yours.

It's much easier for people to pull you away from God than for you to bring them closer to Him.

It's been said that you are the average of the five people you spend the most time with.[1] This suggests your five closest friends have the most influence on your behaviors and attitudes and ultimately shape the person you become. If this is true, we need to be a lot more careful about who we allow to get close to us. If you're not surrounding yourself with Christians, because your faith is a personal thing, just between you and Jesus, you might be inviting trouble.

By contrast, look what Scripture says about walking with people who have wisdom: "Walk with the wise and become wise, for a companion of fools suffers harm" (Proverbs 13:20). The Bible clearly instructs us to walk with wise people, because they are going to have a significant impact on who we become.

And if you truly want to become a person who loves God and is close to Him, then you must make it a priority to get around people who also love Him. (We will be digging into healthy friendships a lot more in the next chapter.)

The times I was falling into sin the most were when I was around people who didn't have a problem with the sin I was committing. It was almost as if I'd bond with a friend over our common sin. We'd laugh together and say we'd do better next time, only to both fall into the same trap of temptation again. We'd get drunk together, all the while laughing in the bars, saying, "Jesus would sit with sinners too."

I would even confess to friends about the sin struggles I was falling into, and some would say, "Ashley, that's not even a big deal." But in those moments, I didn't need someone to dismiss my confession. I needed a *godly* friend to listen, pray for me, and call me higher. And the issue is, not every friend is like that.

If you want to live a life free of temptation, it's important to surround yourself with friends who respect your values and share your commitment to following God. You're going to need accountability on this journey. And if you're close with people who have no reverence for what the Bible says, it will lead you away from God instead of closer to Him.

7. Let God Take the Desire Away

I remember when I was struggling with partying, I would go to bars with the goal of drinking one drink. (And yes, I was underage.) After that first drink, I couldn't resist ordering another one.

The next day, I'd always feel so much shame. No matter how hard I tried, I couldn't shake this sin. I didn't have the willpower to change my behavior.

But that is the problem: We target the behavior. We say we will start reading our Bible every day. We say we will break up with our boyfriend who we know, deep down, we are settling for. We say we will quit hitting the snooze button a million times in the morning. Or stop partying.

Yet targeting the behavior is simply not the way to achieve lasting change.

In *The Power to Change,* Craig Groeschel says, "If you try to change your behavior without changing your identity, you're pulling up a weed without getting to the root."[2] It's kind of like putting a Band-Aid on a cut. Sure, that bandage might stop the bleeding and cover up the injury, but the actual healing must occur deep in the wound. When it comes to our sins, it's easy to just deal with what's on the surface and hide the behavior, while ignoring the deeper problems that might be hard to recognize.

Instead of trying to change the behavior, we must go deeper. We must change the way we see ourselves. We must begin to see ourselves as children of God and let the Word of God shape our worldview. Romans 12:2 advises us, "Don't copy the behavior and customs of this world, but let God transform you into a new person by changing the way you think" (NLT).

Groeschel talks about cybernetics theory in his book, explaining how scientists explored two methods to bring about change in people. The first method is called first-order change, or behavior modification. This might lead to quick results, but the researchers found that it didn't lead to lasting change. The second method is called second order change and focuses on changing the way you think rather than how you act. They discovered that this approach was the only one that truly made a lasting difference.[3]

Isn't it wild when you see the Bible match up with science? Clearly there is a Creator behind this strategy, and we humans are just catching up to what He's already created.

The problem with my drinking was that I still saw myself as the party girl from college. I enjoyed being the one who had fun, dressed for the bars, and loved the loud music. I needed to change my self-image and start seeing myself as a woman of God. Women of God don't party or wear revealing clothes that are admired in clubs, because their worth is no longer tied to these things.

Once I committed to reading the Bible every day and started letting God shape the way I saw myself, I stopped having an urge to go to the bars. That party girl wasn't who I was anymore. After spending time with God and reading what He says about me in the Bible, I knew that He was calling me to walk as one of His children. I knew that I was set apart for His glory. I knew that He had a good plan for me to be a leader and to walk as a godly woman.

The more you let God change the way you see yourself and the more you let the Word of God change the way you see the world, the more you will notice change in your life.

It all starts with letting God change our thoughts.

If you want to be completely transformed from the inside out, pray this with me:

> Father God, I pray that You would reveal to me how You see me and how You created me. I want You and Your Word to

shape the way I see myself and the world You have me in. I want to follow You. Amen.

Stay Faithful Through Temptation

Maybe you are feeling hopeless because no matter how hard you try, you keep falling down.

The Sowing Season is about choosing to get up, even after you fall down. On this side of heaven, we all will mess up.

We will do something we shouldn't do. We will hurt someone we love. We will fall back into the same old sin habits that we are begging to get out of, and there will be times when we feel chained to a struggle we can't shake.

But God is faithful. He is so very faithful to help you out of this struggle with temptation.

And when you get knocked down, you must make the decision to get up and try again, this time with God.

If you have recently fallen into sin and you have believed the lie that God can't forgive you, let me just take a moment to cancel that lie over you in the mighty name of Jesus.

You are an overcomer, through Jesus Christ (Galatians 2:20). No weapon formed against you shall succeed (Isaiah 54:17). His mercies are new every morning (Lamentations 3:23). And if you have repented and decided not to go back to that sin, God has already forgotten about it (Isaiah 43:25).

God Is Quick to Forgive Your Sins

After that bachelorette trip, I felt so much shame. I cried in my room, pleading for the Lord to forgive me. I felt He would always be upset with me because of how I had fallen into sin.

But God was kind, and by His Holy Spirit, He reminded me that as soon as I repented, He had already forgotten about it.

As soon as I turned away from my sin and toward God—and chose to live a life that would honor Him instead of getting drunk—He had already moved on. He had forgotten my sin, just as Hebrews 8:12 says: "I will forgive their wickedness and will remember their sins no more."

Why do we beat ourselves up over things that God has simply already forgotten about? I had to believe that God had forgiven me, and I had to receive His forgiveness for my sins. Only then could I move forward in the peace and joy He was wanting to give me.

Growing with God doesn't look like getting it perfect 100 percent of the time. It looks like choosing to follow God the best we can and letting Him refine us and shape us into the people He always intended for us to be.

When we face temptation, we will receive His grace and strength to overcome it. We will confess and pray with friends who will call us higher, so we will be healed. And we will choose to repent and try again with God, as many times as we need, because His grace is limitless.

And as we take steps with Him each day, we won't want to return to our old sin anymore. The temptation will eventually become a distant memory—because the peace that comes with following God will be better than doing things any other way.

4

Navigating the Wilderness of Loneliness

BEING FAITHFUL IN FRIENDSHIP

When I was in high school, a friend invited me to stay at her lake house for the summer. As I unpacked, I happened to overhear a conversation taking place over speaker phone between my friend and one of our mutual friends. To my shock, the mutual friend began to talk badly about me.

Tears welled in my eyes as I stared at my summer dresses laid out on the hardwood floor. Was this the first time my friends had talked about me? Why did it sound like they'd done this before?

I wish I could say this was an isolated event, but it was one of countless times when I felt discouraged in a friendship. Whether because of being intentionally excluded, mistreated, or made to be the subject of gossip, I often felt like the odd one out during my high school years.

When I started my relationship with God, my sense of

being left out became even worse. Despite my newfound joy in having Jesus in my life, I somehow felt more alone in my friendships. Since few of my friends at the time were Christian, not many of them could understand the life-changing transformation I had experienced. I also had absolutely no clue how to make good Christian friends who could help me grow closer to God and become who He created me to be. And with my difficult friendship history, I was worried I would never find good, Jesus-centered friends.

You can probably relate. Maybe you've been the girl who never received invites to those parties. Or the girl who felt like she was never enough, because her friends constantly pointed out her flaws or insecurities. Or the girl who was more on the fringes of her friend group than in the center of it. Maybe you've struggled to go deep with friends who don't share your life of faith or encourage you to grow closer to God. Maybe you consider yourself introverted, shy, or scared to talk to people. Maybe you deeply desire godly, lifelong friends—people you can cry with, laugh with, talk with—but you're just not sure how to get there. Whatever your friendship journey has looked like, know this: You are not alone in feeling alone.

We'll explore all of that in this chapter: what the Bible says about Christian friends and how to find the friends God has planned for you. We'll explore how to be faithful and sow seeds in friendships, and we'll create a vision for how to harvest a bountiful community of good friends.

Friendship Shifts

At this point, you might be thinking, *Ashley, you have no idea how hard it is for me. I've tried to make new friends, but all my efforts feel one-sided.* Or, *I'm too scared to approach new people. What if they reject me?* Or, *My best friend isn't a Christian, but we've been through everything together. Is it really that big of a deal if she's not as close to God as I am?*

While I might not know your current situation, I can empathize with feeling insecurity and fear in forging new friendships. Making friends isn't always easy, and maintaining those friendships can be just as hard. You might finally click with someone, only for them to move away, get a new job, start a new relationship, or even shift their hobbies or priorities. Those moments are hard, especially when they signal an end to a friendship you had hoped would last. But forcing a friendship to work isn't going to help you or the other person. And it might even prevent both of you from discovering life-giving friendships God could have in store for you.

Over the years, I've found that God gives us some relationships that last a lifetime. These friendships are rare and sacred. Other relationships last only for a season, and that's okay too. These friendships might even be sweeter because they are brief. Or perhaps they have to end because they would otherwise cause us harm.

Sometimes God draws certain people closer to us while allowing others to drift further away. Instead of resisting that, we can try to see the new relationships He brings into our lives as gifts. And instead of grieving what we once had, we can choose to embrace what beautiful things He has for us right now.

Red and Green Flags

Before we identify the qualities of a good friend, let's explore what a good friend is not. If you notice a friend exhibiting any of these red flags, consider having a hard conversation, setting up a boundary, or even taking a step back:

- gossips frequently
- has a rude or unkind attitude
- excludes you or others
- discourages or demoralizes you or others
- engages in other toxic behavior
- consistently coaxes you away from following God's Word

In the gospel of Matthew, Jesus offers this advice: "Beware of false prophets who come disguised as harmless sheep but are really vicious wolves. You can identify them by their fruit, that is, by the way they act" (7:15–16, NLT). When searching for godly friendships, we should pay attention to a person's fruit—their actions. If their words and actions don't align, consider that a warning of the person's true character. With that in mind, pay attention to these more specific types of red flags:

- They say they love you—but they gossip about you behind your back.
- They say they will always be there for you—but they don't show up for you when you really need it.
- They say Jesus is the most important part of their life—but their actions on the weekend don't show it.

No matter what someone says, their fruit will truly show whether they have been transformed by Christ. If they are mean and exclusive and toxic, be careful how much you open up to them, even if they say they're a believer. This isn't to say that a true follower of Jesus will be perfect, but their actions and words should hint at how they're growing closer to God and becoming more like Jesus.

On that note, let's take a look at green flags in friendship, particularly through the lens of Christianity. Good, Christ-centered friends . . .

- are faithful (Proverbs 27:6)
- are without anger (Proverbs 22:24)
- stick closer than a brother (Proverbs 18:24)
- encourage and build each other up (1 Thessalonians 5:11)
- help each other (Ecclesiastes 4:9–10)
- are wise (Proverbs 13:20)
- love at all times (Proverbs 17:17)
- are kind (Matthew 7:12)

Keep in mind that none of us are perfect and even the strongest Christians will fail to live up to this list. So rather than rigidly holding to these traits and unfriending anyone who misses one (because we all will), try to treat this list more as a guideline. And overall, remember that a godly friend will bring good fruit into your life. A helpful question to consider in your friendships is this: *Does this friend bring me closer to God or further away?*

When Your Friends Aren't Christian

If those in your immediate circle consistently discourage or demean your faith, staying on fire for God can be challenging. Even if you aren't being ridiculed for your faith, you might still struggle if you don't have anyone intentionally *encouraging* you to draw closer to God. If that's the case for you, I want you to know that you are not alone.

In high school, when I found out about Jesus, none of my friends had much faith at all. They would even make fun of Christians. After I became a believer, I struggled to resist the party scene and the things I was doing with my boyfriend, because my friends were doing all the same things. I didn't want to be the odd one out. I also didn't want to have *no* friends just because I had decided to follow Jesus.

Unfortunately, this kind of self-preservationist thinking led me to become lukewarm in my faith. Because I was so afraid of being alone or ostracized, I chose to stick close to people who didn't put God first. Looking back now, ten years later, I know this was a mistake. If I had instead chosen to trust God with my life *and* my friendships, I have no doubt He would have led me to good and healthy Christian friends.

In Paul's second letter to the Corinthian church, he warns believers not to be "yoked" to unbelievers (6:14). Although he is specifically talking about marriage in this passage, being yoked (coupled with or attached to) can also be used in reference to the way we connect to others in friendships.

You shouldn't be attached to every person you meet. I have many friends that I love, but I wouldn't consider myself coupled with them. Thankfully, I do have a few people in my life who are very, very close to me. My best friend, Ally, and I live together, and she's basically my right hand. Fortunately for me, she's also a very strong believer, and her presence in my life is always an encouragement to my own walk with Jesus.

As Christians, our goal should never be to surround ourselves only with other believers or cut off anyone who doesn't love Jesus. The gospel would never make it past the church doors if we did that! But when it comes to those we call our closest friends, we should make sure they share a love for Jesus. Because we will become like whoever we spend most of our time with. So if the friends in your immediate circle are always partying all weekend or convincing you to do the types of things the Holy Spirit has been convicting you *not* to do, then maybe you need to take a step back and reevaluate how much time you spend with them.

Believe me, I know definitive decisions like this are hard—especially if *all* your friends tend to fall into the "bad influence" category. But you can still be a good friend to them and show them the love of Jesus while putting up some healthy boundaries so you can remain true to your values. You can also start being more intentional with making new friends by faithfully showing up to church, Bible studies, or other faith-centered events that will introduce you to people who share your values. Again, this is hard work and will likely take you through some ups and downs, but the rewards will be worth it.

Of course, solid Christian friendships don't just happen overnight. Depending on your situation, you might suddenly end up with a lot of solo time on your calendar, and that's okay. After Paul's encounter with Jesus on the road to Damascus, he spent *three years* studying the Scriptures on his own before embarking on his missionary journeys (Galatians 1:15–18). Following his example, try to see this in-between time as an opportunity to grow closer to Jesus. Treat these free weekends and nights alone as chances to dive into God's Word and to deepen your faith. Moments like these are never wasted.

I cultivated these types of habits during my post-grad years. Instead of going out to bars on the weekends, I declined those invites and either hung out with people from my church or spent time alone with God. Surprisingly, those solitary evenings didn't feel lonely. As I studied the Word and listened to worship music, I experienced the fullness of God's presence.

The same can happen for you too. I know a season of trying to make new friends can be lonely, but a beautiful thing happens when you choose to not live a life of compromise and to fully commit to Jesus. You get to experience the indescribable peace and comfort of knowing you are not alone and will never be alone, since Jesus is at your side.

As Iron Sharpens Iron

But Ashley, you might be saying, *my friends may not be Christian, but they're not into the party scene either. Even though I have a different faith from them, we still have so much in common and I can't imagine them being a bad influence on me or tempting me to do things I know are wrong.*

Hear me clearly: Friends who will support your beliefs and values even if they don't share them are truly a gift. Even better if they will hold space for you to explain how your life is being transformed through Christ.

However, I would still challenge you to be intentional with finding friends who are fellow believers and who can spur you on to deepen your walk with God. Having only non-Christian friends will limit you from stepping into the life of purpose God has called you to. These friends may even drain your passion for God.

Being around people that drain me never has a good effect on my walk with God. As much as I don't want the people I spend time with to rub off on me, they always will. Proverbs 27:17 says, "As iron sharpens iron, so one person sharpens another." In other words, especially when you're a new Christian, you should aim to surround yourself with fellow believers who will sharpen your faith and your relationship with Jesus.

Are your friends sharpening your walk with God or dulling it? Are those in your immediate circle challenging you to deepen your faith or making it easy for you to just skate by?

Let's be real. Finding new friends is much more difficult

than simply sticking with the ones you already have. Hitting up the same group chats and attending the same events you've always attended is much easier than trying out new environments where you don't know a single soul. Accepting an invite to a party or movie is much more convenient than going to a new Bible study or worship night on your own. What if no one talks to you? What if you get rejected?

Hopefully, you won't get rejected, since church communities tend to be very welcoming spaces, but all Christ-followers are still human and will make mistakes. So, if you do experience any awkwardness or other discomfort when building a new community of believers, have patience with yourself and with them. As difficult as it is to put yourself out there, the challenges will serve to strengthen you and make *you* a better friend. More importantly, God will always find a way to meet you when you step out in faith into new environments.

The Fruit of Church Community

So how do you find a good Christian community? Well, one of the best ways is through the local church. But let me just tell you that, in my experience, finding a church in a new city isn't always easy.

I recently moved to Los Angeles. As with any move, I had to start over and find my footing, as well as a new faith community where I could plant roots and grow. Almost right away, Ally and I got really involved in a ministry we had connected with before our move. We became close friends with the leaders of the ministry and spent a lot of time with them.

But then the ministry moved to another state. And it was like we had to start over from ground zero.

At first, Ally and I debated whether we should have gone with the ministry to the other state. We prayed about it and really sought God's wisdom. But as we prayed, we felt God remind us that He had brought us to Los Angeles and we hadn't come here just to up and leave. God wanted us to be planted where He had sent us. And that would mean staying in California.

The decision was difficult and lonely at first. Our entire community was now gone. At one point, Ally was one of only two friends I had in California.

But as the loneliness set in, I felt the Lord impress on my heart that we needed to find a church. We were on our own, we didn't really have any mentors or other people to go to for guidance, and we didn't have many brothers and sisters in Christ. The result was that I felt more and more homesick.

I talked with Ally, and we made a plan to intentionally find a church home in L.A. We prayed that God would guide us to the right church and to the right community—a community that would feel like home.

And then we started googling. As we prowled the internet for churches in Los Angeles, I kept seeing the same one pop up. During that time, I felt led to watch a YouTube vlog posted by a girl who used to live in California. In the vlog, she was visiting her old church, which just happened to be the same church that had been popping up for me.

I texted Ally: *Ally. I think we need to go to this church.*

Shortly after that, our friend Carew said, "Also, can we

all go to this church tomorrow?" He sent a link to the same church that had been on my radar.

God was speaking. For some reason, all the arrows were pointing toward this one church.

On Sunday, Ally and I walked through the church doors with our friend Carew, not knowing a soul. Yet it immediately felt like home. The pastor even prayed for us the very first time we went.

Months later, Ally and I now have mentors, attend a Bible study with other women, and are known and loved by a group of people who have made this city that once felt like a foreign land finally feel like home.

I'm so grateful Ally and I didn't just stay in our safe bubble and keep our same old routines. I'm also so grateful we didn't give up on this city. Because it was clear God still had more for us out here than we even realized. He had a home for us to be accepted into, a place where we would belong.

Going Alone

As hard as finding a church in L.A. was, I know doing it by myself would have been even harder. I'm so blessed that I had Ally with me every step of the way. But I know that isn't always true. We don't always have a built-in buddy with us when doing the hard things or taking new steps of faith. Sometimes we must go it alone.

When I previously moved to Nashville, I didn't really know anyone at all. I had my brother, but that was about it. To make friends and find people who truly loved Jesus, I knew I had to find a church. And that meant going to church alone.

So—multiple times—I went to church alone, walked in alone, and sat alone. I felt like everyone and their mother were staring at me as I dared to go into these spaces of communal worship by myself. But each time I went to a new church, I would ask God to go with me. And He always did.

After several weeks of trying out churches, I still hadn't found a spiritual home. But my online ministry was getting bigger, and I knew I needed a spiritual covering and a spiritual family to support me on my own faith journey.

Spiritual covering refers to the biblical concept of submitting to the authority of a more mature Christian leader, typically a pastor or elder, who provides guidance, accountability, and protection over your spiritual life. This person essentially acts as a shield against spiritual attacks by offering prayer and counsel. First Peter 5:5 says, "You who are younger, submit yourselves to your elders. All of you, clothe yourselves with humility toward one another, because, 'God opposes the proud but shows favor to the humble.' "

So as awkward as I felt walking into these churches alone, I asked the Lord to help me find the right community and to reveal to me the right church to be planted in.

After just a couple of months of looking, He did.

At the time, I had an intern who was helping me with my social media. She told me about a church called Harvest Sound and explained how—despite being small—it felt like a family and was the absolute best church she had ever found in Nashville. I decided to go and check it out.

This time when I walked through the church doors, I saw

my friend there. Then I was given a welcome bag, which included a free coffee at the church coffee shop. (God knew how to reach my heart!) I also met a girl named Emily, who smiled from ear to ear and asked for my number.

As I sat through the service, a warm vanilla latte in my hand, I was comforted by the love and warmth of the spiritual family around me. The worship felt like a hug, and the message hit home. The church was no more than a hundred people, but it was like a tight-knit family. Almost like I was a stranger who had walked in on a close family dinner but who had been completely welcomed and made to feel at home.

And it didn't stop there.

My new friend Emily invited me to post-church brunch at Chipotle. I was nervous to go, but of course I said yes. And when I sat down with my bowl, I saw that around fifteen other people in their twenties were joining as well. In fact, the table where I was sitting got so crowded that our group started another table.

For the first time in a long time, I felt seen and surrounded by people who loved Jesus. The church felt not just like a building but like a solid community who really cared to know me. I knew then that God had led me to the right church.

Over the next year, I partnered with that church to reach the young people of Nashville. I got to know new friends, went to weddings, received prayer and spiritual encouragement, and finally felt like I had found my very first church home. It was also this church that sent me out to my next mission in California.

I share these stories to show that when you ask God to lead you to the right places, the right communities, the right *church,* and when you dare to take a step of faith when you feel like He is guiding you in a certain direction, He will be faithful to reward you. He will lead you to exactly where you need to be. I'm always encouraged by Isaiah 58:11: "The LORD will guide you continually, giving you water when you are dry and restoring your strength. You will be like a well-watered garden, like an ever-flowing spring" (NLT).

Getting out of your house may not be the easiest thing. I know you might be lonely, and I know you might be dreading leaving your comfort zone and walking into church buildings alone. But I want to encourage you to ask the Lord, right now, to lead you to the community He knows you need. Then I want you to just start going to churches that you feel the Lord is leading you to.

Listen, you might not always feel like getting out of your house by yourself or going to church, Bible studies, or that one ministry on your own. Did I feel like going to all those churches by myself? Absolutely not. But just because you don't feel like doing something doesn't mean you shouldn't do it.

Decide now to choose the hard thing over the easy thing. You will get out of your house, and you won't use being introverted as an excuse to be alone or separated from Christian community. Whether you're extroverted or introverted—you need people. You need a church family.

In Acts, we see the first body of believers gathering together *every day.* Acts 2:46–47 says, "Every day they continued to meet together in the temple courts. They broke bread in their homes and ate together with glad and sincere hearts, praising God and enjoying the favor of all the people.

And the Lord added to their number daily those who were being saved." I can imagine if they were around today, they would make their way to Chipotle a few times over.

Finding Sisters in Christ

Once you find your church community, how can you go deeper in your relationships? How do you find those incredible, unmatched, go-to-for-everything sisters in Christ?

So many of my followers are constantly asking me, "How do I find my Christian best friend?"

As a first step, let's revisit what we covered in the last section: Go to church, get connected to believers, and be involved in the church community. Even if you have to go alone. Even if you have to attend that small group alone. Even if you have to go to that worship night alone. Remember, you are never truly alone, because God is always with you.

I love what Joshua 1:9 says: "Have I not commanded you? Be strong and courageous. Do not be afraid; do not be discouraged, for the LORD your God will be with you wherever you go."

We can't ask God for community but stay in our safe little comfort zones. As you pray for God to lead you to the friends He has for you, He may give you opportunities to step out of your comfort zone and go to places where that community is. You might get invited to a Bible study, to a service at church, to a post-church brunch, or maybe even to a school ministry gathering. Whatever it is, when the invitation shows up—

choose to be bold and go. Even if it's completely out of your comfort zone.

God rewards those who step out in faith and trust Him. He sees you making the brave decision, and He will meet you there. Just keep in mind that He can't always meet you if you don't first step out.

Do It Afraid

I think many of us believe that being afraid to do something is a sign we shouldn't do it. If something feels too hard or uncomfortable, we use that as an excuse not to do it. But in many aspects of my life—and especially in my walk with Jesus—I've found the opposite to be true. Sometimes doing the hard thing is exactly what God is calling you to. Sometimes, even if something feels scary, you're still supposed to do it.

If you're an introvert, this message might feel especially challenging, but this truth applies to everyone. To those who prefer to be homebodies. To those who are shy. To those who feel like no matter which space they enter, they simply don't belong.

Staying in your comfort zone is always going to be easier. But that doesn't mean it will be better, especially in the long run. After all, you won't forge lifelong connections or a solid Christian community by staying in your house. So be bold and get out there, even if you're scared. Do it while you're afraid. Because God is on your side. And with Him walking with you, you don't need to fear anything.

Matthew 14 tells a story of when the disciples were sailing across a lake in the dark hours of the morning. When they saw something that looked like a ghost, they became terrified and cried out in fear, completely freaking out. They didn't know that what they thought was a ghost was actually just Jesus.

Thankfully, Jesus responded to their fear: "Take courage! It is I. Don't be afraid" (verse 27).

Then the disciple Peter, being the fearless person he was, said, "Lord, if it's you . . . tell me to come to you on the water" (verse 28).

Jesus said, "Come" (verse 29).

> Then Peter got down out of the boat, walked on the water and came toward Jesus. But when he saw the wind, he was afraid and, beginning to sink, cried out, "Lord, save me!"
>
> Immediately Jesus reached out his hand and caught him. "You of little faith," he said, "why did you doubt?" (verses 29–31)

Peter was able to do the miraculous when he was looking at Jesus. But the very moment he took his eyes off God, he sank.

When you enter new or uncomfortable or even scary places, try to keep in mind this story of Peter. As you do the brave thing—especially if you're doing it alone—fix your gaze on Jesus. When you do, you will be clothed with peace. You can even ask the Holy Spirit to help you focus on God the entire time.

When I was in college and had to go places alone, I would

be so nervous. But then I would ask for the Holy Spirit's help, and I would feel the Lord say, "Ash, just focus on Me!" So I would follow His lead, and I would forget that I was even afraid in the first place.

The Scriptures back this up as well. In Isaiah 26:3, God promises He will give us His perfect peace when our thoughts are centered on Him, *because* we trust in Him. The Bible also instructs us to fix our gaze on Jesus in Hebrews 12: "Let us run with perseverance the race marked out for us, fixing our eyes on Jesus, the pioneer and perfecter of faith" (verses 1–2).

I used to wonder what it means to fix my eyes on Jesus. Did I need to go into these places looking up at Jesus and running into people the whole time? After more study, I realized that it means to fix my *focus* on God.

Fixing your eyes on Jesus very simply means looking away from other things and focusing your attention on Jesus. It means relying on Him for help and encouragement. It means turning away from things that might distract you, like people-pleasing, fears, and insecurities. When you fix your gaze on Jesus, you can walk on water. Because, ultimately, you are trusting God completely, which puts you in the perfect position to see Him come through in an incredible way.

The minute you focus on other things like your circumstances or what people may think of you, you begin to sink. When Peter lost his trust in Jesus, that was when he began to sink. But when Jesus told him not to doubt that He truly had his back, He reminded Peter to shift his focus back to Jesus.

In the same way, when you walk into new places alone, have faith that God is going to hold your hand and go with you. He will help you walk into these places and make it to the other side. Don't worry about what people will think of you or what the outcome will be. Simply trust the Lord, who knows what will come from every step of faith.

So, no more excuses. Step out of your house. Greet those around you. Accept that invitation. Get planted in a church. Even if you have to do it afraid. When you keep showing up, not giving up until you find community, you will eventually be able to look back and realize that God's hand was with you the whole time. And that He led you to exactly where you need to be.

How to Start a Conversation

So you've done the hard thing by showing up in a new space with the hope of meeting other believers. Now what do you do? You could just sit in the back and keep to yourself until the moment when you can slip out unnoticed. But you could accomplish the same thing by sitting on your couch and watching a sermon online. Remember, you won't find a solid Christian community if you don't put yourself out there. But realistically and practically, how do you meet new people? How should you start a conversation when you don't know a single soul?

No doubt you've been around people who talk way too much. The type of people who become the center of attention the moment they walk into a room. The type of people who don't let anyone else get a word in as they talk a mile a minute. Interestingly, the Bible warns us about this. Proverbs 10:19

very bluntly says, "Too much talk leads to sin. Be sensible and keep your mouth shut" (NLT).

Keeping this wise proverb in mind, try to reorient your perspective when you walk into new spaces. Instead of worrying what other people will think of you or wondering how you can best impress others, go in with the intention of getting to know someone else and of helping someone else be seen. Instead of talking all about yourself, *ask questions* and genuinely listen to their answer.

To put it simply, here's what you can do: Ask the Lord to lead you to the right person with whom you can strike up conversation. See which person your eye is drawn to in a crowd. Then go up to that person, say hello, introduce yourself, and ask them a question. Not only will this show that you care and let the other person feel heard, but it will also allow you to be better prepared for the conversation. If you're the one coming with the question, you'll know ahead of time what the topic will be. You won't have to worry about doing all the talking. And you'll also learn about the other person, make them feel seen and loved, and see if this could be a good friend.

I've made asking questions and listening a regular habit when I meet others, and people often say, "Oh my goodness—Ashley is the *nicest* person ever. Literally so kind." And guess what? I rarely say anything in those interactions. Hardly any words at all. All I do is ask questions and listen so the other person feels welcomed and loved.

Don't diminish the power of listening to others. In *American Gangster,* a movie starring Denzel Washington, his character Frank Lucas says this powerful line: "The loudest one in the room is the weakest one in the room."[1] Listening conveys security and confidence because you aren't anxiously filling every silence with words. Listening helps you focus on serving the other person, which allows you to shine the light of Jesus. Listening also gets you out of your own head.

Jesus set the example of being a listener. He often asked questions and listened carefully to the answers. By doing the same, we can be His hands and feet. Matthew 20:26–28 says, "Whoever wants to become great among you must be your servant, and whoever wants to be first must be your slave—just as the Son of Man did not come to be served, but to serve, and to give his life as a ransom for many."

So, as you step into new places to meet new people, keep your eyes on Jesus. Focus on asking questions, listening, and *serving* the person in front of you. However you would want this person to treat you, do so to them. This is a much better place to put your energy than trying to get the other person to like you.

Be the Friend You Want to Have

All humans—but especially women—struggle with worrying too much about what others think of them. As a result, we end up with a lot of pressure on ourselves. Pressure to look a certain way, talk a certain way, and *be* a certain way—all so we can impress the people around us (who are probably also thinking more about themselves than they are about us). But what would it look like if we removed that weight from ourselves?

Because I experienced a lot of exclusion in middle school, I arrived in high school with pretty bad social anxiety. I would sit at the lunch table and feel so anxious that I would struggle to get any words out at all.

Fear was keeping me from making good relationships. I was way too worried about how people felt about me. So in any social interactions, all I could do was focus on myself, wondering what people thought of me and whether I was making a good impression.

These insecurities became especially noticeable during sorority recruitment. As I went from one house to another, all I could think about was what other people were thinking about me. Each time I did this, I never really acted like myself and could barely get any words out. It was self-sabotage at its finest. In an attempt to get others to like me, I wasn't even acting like myself at all.

It's super easy to walk into spaces and be inward focused, thinking only about ourselves. Carrying trauma or having a history of being excluded can make us even more self-conscious and aware of how others feel about us. And we can become extra sensitive and defensive if we're worried people don't like us.

During my sorority recruitment, I could have kept spiraling deeper into myself and losing the unique parts of me that make me who I am. But instead, I reached a moment when I shifted the focus off myself and onto how I could be a friend to the person in front of me. When I did that, I began to enjoy the experience. Not only that, but I was also able to be more like myself, rather than pretending to be someone I thought other people would like. With my attention off myself, I could place it on loving and serving others. I could refocus on God. One of my mentors described this phenomenon to me as being "God-centered, others-focused."

I love this beautiful quote from C. S. Lewis:

> Give up yourself, and you will find your real self. Lose your life and you will save it. Submit to death, death of your ambitions and favourite wishes every day and death of your whole body in the end: submit with every fibre of your being, and you will find eternal life. Keep back nothing. Nothing that you have not given away will be really yours. Nothing in you that has not died will ever be raised from the dead. Look for yourself, and you will find in the long run only hatred, loneliness, despair, rage, ruin, and decay. But look for Christ and you will find Him, and with Him everything else thrown in.[2]

Because God created us to live in freedom by having our minds set on Him, the more we focus on ourselves, the more anxious and miserable we end up being. But when we look to Christ and set our hearts on serving others, we actually become the truest version of ourselves. The more we focus on loving God and loving others, the more peace and joy we feel. And the less we think about ourselves, the freer we are.

So as you build up your community of fellow believers, focus on being the kind of person you want to talk to. Notice others more than yourself. And be the friend you want to have.

Friends Who Speak Life

In His time on earth, Jesus spent time with people from all walks of life—lowly fishermen, women, lepers, children, and other outcasts. But He also had a smaller group of close followers that He spent most of His time with. And He knew the importance of spending time directly with God.

We are not Jesus, so how much more do we need to spend time with God and with other people who love Him!

Just the other week, I was having one of the worst days I'd had in a long time. I'd cried myself to sleep the previous night. And of course, feeling the way I did, in complete despair and with puffy eyes, I didn't want to socialize. Unfortunately, some people from my church had organized a Super Bowl party that I'd been planning to attend. As I sat in my car, having just sobbed my eyes out, I wondered if I should even go. But somehow I felt the Spirit of God tell me that the very last thing I should do in that moment was be alone. He reminded me that I was going to be with my friends from church, which is just about the best and safest group to be with whenever I have a bad day.

So, I went into that party with puffy red eyes. I don't know if people could tell I'd been crying, but I ended up sharing with two friends at the party how I was really feeling. By the grace of God, they'd been feeling like something was up with me too. They have the Holy Spirit, and the Holy Spirit has a beautiful way of giving us the discernment to see when someone needs to be encouraged.

I cried to those two friends on the couch at the Super Bowl

party, and they prayed over me, listened to God with me, and encouraged me in my sadness. After talking with them both, I felt so much more encouraged. It was almost like a weight had been lifted off me.

When I got home, I called a mentor of mine from church, who is just a few years older than me. She also spoke life and hope into the situation I was in. Together, we ended up rebuking the lies I'd been believing. By the end of the night, I felt like a completely new person. All because I fought the desire to be alone in my sorrow.

If I hadn't gone to the party and opened up to my friends, I wouldn't have felt the weight lift off. If I hadn't humbled myself and asked for help from a mentor I trust and love, I wouldn't have been able to identify the lies I was believing or receive the truth that God wanted to give me. Much of the day's breakthrough and healing came from the community God had given me. They enabled me to stand firm against the enemy's schemes in what felt like an emotional hurricane.

As I experienced that night, we can't do life alone. We need a church family. We need spiritual brothers and sisters in Christ to do life with, spiritual fathers and mothers to look after us, and close Christian friends to share the most intimate parts of our hearts with. We need people who are running the same path we are to help us grow closer to God.

So, if you're tired of feeling alone, of being easily influenced by those you're hanging out with, or of feeling too anxious or nervous to go to church in person, remember this: Nothing changes if nothing changes. I know this because I experienced the same struggles. And things didn't begin to turn around until I admitted I needed people in my life who were going to do this Christian life with me.

God wants good friendships for you too. In fact, your closest Jesus-loving friends might be right around the corner, even if you haven't met them yet. Know that Jesus is cheering you on as you go on this journey. You can simply ask God to provide your community and then step out to find it.

A Prayer for Finding Friends

We aren't going to find good Christian friendships without praying for them. I think one of the reasons I was able to find community and friends in the new cities I've lived in is that I fervently prayed that God would lead me.

If you've been praying, don't stop. God loves persistent prayer, and He hears you.

I love how the book of James talks about the power of prayer. James 5:16 says this: "Confess your sins to each other and pray for each other so that you may be healed. The earnest prayer of a righteous person has great power and produces wonderful results" (NLT).

Sometimes in our loneliest moments, we can feel like God isn't anywhere near us and isn't listening to our cries. But it's in those moments when we feel so alone, so lost, and so hopeless that He is closest to us. He is near to the brokenhearted. And He answers those who cry to Him for help (Psalm 34:17–18).

If you are really in a lonely season and you desire kingdom friendships, ask the Lord to guide you to the friends He knows you need. Ask Him to provide good friends in your life to draw you closer to Jesus. He cares about this prayer of your heart. And He wants to provide for all your needs—even this one.

Ask God to help you find friends. Ask Him to show you a Bible study. Ask Him to lead you to a church family of brothers and sisters in Christ you can do life with—who will know you, love you, and encourage you to run your race with the Lord.

Let's pray this prayer together:

> Jesus, I know You don't want me to live this life alone. I humbly admit my need for the right community and right friendships that are going to lead me closer to You. Abba, I ask that You would provide the Christian friendships You know I need and lead me to the right church to be planted in. Make it so obvious that I can't miss it. Help me serve in the community You plant me in. Thank You in advance for leading me to the right people, Lord. In Jesus's name, amen.

5

Trusting in God's Timing

BEING FAITHFUL IN SINGLENESS

I've been single a lot longer than I thought I would be.

I was always the type of girl who hopped from one relationship to another. Even as I was breaking up with one boyfriend, I was already scheming on who I would be with next. This pattern continued from the time I was sixteen until I was twenty-one, when my boyfriend of four years and I parted ways.

After that breakup, I was sure I would date someone else soon. But God had other plans. I ended up falling in love with God and leaving my old lukewarm lifestyle fully in the past.

A year went by, and I thought that surely the man God had for me would come soon.

Another year went by. This time, I did a twenty-one-day fast. No man yet.

Another year went by. This time, I moved to a new city. Surely *now* he would come soon.

Another year went by. I wasn't really meeting anyone who could be the one.

Another year went by. This time, I was just about to release a book about being in a waiting season. Surely, after this book launched, he would come.

And another year went by. By now I'm completely and utterly confused. *Where is he? Why am I still single?*

Sometimes Things Don't Make Sense to Us

I never imagined spending all my twenties single. Most of my closest college friends are now married. Many of them are sending me baby shower invitations, already moving on to the next season of life.

Meanwhile, I haven't had a boyfriend in the past six years.

Sometimes things don't make sense. Sometimes God doesn't answer our prayers in the timeline we expected. Sometimes God gives us a dream and that dream takes a very long time to come true.

I've cried countless tears over this aspect of my life. In fact, to be totally transparent, it's one of the hardest areas I've had to navigate. I've wondered whether something is wrong with me, doubted my worth, and even felt tempted to take matters into my own hands and just find a boyfriend myself.

But whenever I feel this way, the Lord reminds me that He has someone for me—and I won't have to force a relationship with that person. It will just come naturally. Our marriage will be a gift from God.

I just don't know when that day will be.

If you're waiting for a spouse, you know how difficult it can be to make the most of where God has you right now. If you're anything like me, a big part of you just wants to put life on pause until you meet that special person.

However, had I paused my life the past six years, I would have missed out on all the incredible experiences and growth that God meant for me in my twenties. I would have missed out on the adventures, the projects, the friendships, and the opportunities to step out of my comfort zone.

In this chapter, we will discuss how to be faithful to the Lord in your singleness, when you're waiting for God to send your spouse. Just because you're waiting doesn't mean this season needs to be wasted.

A Shift of Perspective

Every time I would question God on why I'm still single, He would show me the grass isn't always greener somewhere else.

On one occasion, He brought me into two different conversations. The first was with my friend who has been married for about four years. During a phone call, she confided in me that they were struggling financially, expressing her fear about how they would be able to pay off her husband's debt.

Shortly after, I had a conversation with a friend who had a newborn. She shared her struggles with me, explaining that her husband was often away from home because of work, so he wasn't able to help very much with the baby. She confided that she was struggling to get sleep and raise this child while he was traveling.

In both these instances, the Lord had to show me that other situations aren't necessarily better. It's not as if all your problems just go away when you get married. Marriage can sometimes bring additional challenges because it comes with more weight. You are no longer just an individual; you are connected to another person. And if you have children, you are responsible for even more people.

It's a lot to steward.

I think we often look at married people or people with babies and think they have made it. And while building a life with marriage and babies is beautiful, it doesn't mean it's void of trouble. There truly is no perfect destination on this side of heaven.

Here's the truth: You can be as happy as you want to be, right where God has you.

You don't have to wait to be happy until you have a ring on your finger or a baby on your lap. Those things are great, and they do bring immense joy. But God has good things and much joy for *you*, right where you are right now. Single or married, with kids or not.

Because the truth is, if God wanted us to be with someone, we would be with someone. There is a *reason* He has us single right now.

And we might not be able to see it, but someday we will understand. And until then, we can make the most of the wonderful gifts God has given us, right here, right now.

Make the Most of Where He Has You

God's gifts come in mysterious disguises. The biggest blessings in your life may come from unexpected or challenging situations. God has a beautiful way of turning even the worst of circumstances into something positive.

Sometimes it's tempting to look at where other people are in life and be jealous because of where we *aren't.* But when we do that, we miss out on stewarding what God has put in front of us right now.

It makes me think of the parable of the talents. In this story in Matthew 25:14–30, Jesus describes a master who gave his servants different amounts of gold (talents) and then saw how each one stewarded it. To one servant he gave five talents, to another servant two talents, and to the last servant only one talent.

The servant who received five talents invested it and made five more.

The servant who received two talents invested it and made two more.

But the servant who had only one talent didn't believe it was worth much, so he buried it in the ground.

The master was gravely disappointed with the last servant. So much so that he said, "You wicked, lazy servant!" (verse 26).

He continued, "So take the bag of gold from him and give it to the one who has ten bags. For whoever has will be given more, and they will have an abundance. Whoever does not have, even what they have will be taken from them. And throw that worthless servant outside, into the darkness, where there will be weeping and gnashing of teeth" (verses 28–30).

Many of us are like the guy with one talent. We want to be wives, but we aren't stewarding well the season God has us in. We see those around us who are married with kids, and we think that because we aren't, we should bury our season in the ground until God gives us a spouse. *Then* it will be time to resume our life.

We think life can't move forward, because we have just that one talent. But God is saying He wants us to make the most of what He has given us, *right now.*

No matter where you are, there's a gift waiting to be discovered. You will always be waiting for something. But focusing too much on what you don't have can prevent you from appreciating the gift God has given you already.

God knows exactly what you need, and He knows when you need it. I love Matthew 6:28–30: "Why do you worry about clothes? See how the flowers of the field grow. They do not labor or spin. Yet I tell you that not even Solomon in all his splendor was dressed like one of these. If that is how God clothes the grass of the field, which is here today and tomorrow is thrown into the fire, will he not much more clothe you—you of little faith?"

Someday you might even reflect longingly on this season—when you had all the time in the world—especially during those nights when you're up taking care of your newborn. You just might regret not appreciating this season more.

In the past, to shift my perspective, I would write out all the things God has given me to steward in this season of singleness. Next to each item, I wrote out how I could steward that thing well for God's glory. I called this my "faithfulness chart."

Here's what my list looked like, but I encourage you to make your own:

WHAT GOD HAS GIVEN ME	HOW I CAN BE FAITHFUL WITH IT
My family	I can love my family as Jesus would.
My friendships	I can be a loving and encouraging friend.
My health	I can take care of my body as a temple of the Holy Spirit.
My work	I can do my work with excellence and diligence.
My relationship with God	I can spend time with God and grow closer to Him every day.
My home	I can be a good steward of my home.
My dreams	I can work toward the dreams and visions God gave me.

God wants me to be a faithful steward of everything He has given me. And I can't expect more from Him if I don't steward what I already have. We can all develop our gifts in this season of singleness. This is time we won't ever get back if one day we are married and have kids.

I think about my day off right now. I get to do literally whatever I want. I can wake up as early or as late as I'd like to; I can get a workout in without thinking of childcare; I can go grab a coffee from my favorite coffee shop without needing to coordinate with a husband. I don't have to make my plans around a spouse or kids.

During singleness, you also get to cultivate meaningful relationships with your friends and family. When I'm married with kids, I won't have the time to go to worship nights or Bible studies every day with my friends. I'm also not likely to have the time to love on my extended family as much.

We get to choose to make the most of this season, investing in the gifts God has given us today. And who knows? As you make the most of where you are right now, your husband could be right around the corner.

Look Cute and Pray

The best thing you can do as a woman of God is to *stop looking for a man.*

I *always* used to be looking to see if there were any cute guys in whatever room I was stepping into. At church, I would scan the pews to see if a tall, dark, and handsome man was present. I was on the lookout just about everywhere—at dinner groups, big Bible studies, and other hangouts.

I was looking for a man . . . but the Lord wanted me to be found.

Proverbs 18:22 really helped change my perspective on this: "The man who finds a wife finds a treasure, and he receives favor from the LORD" (NLT).

You, my sister, are meant to be *found.* You are not to be the one looking. God made you to be the treasure, the prize worth finding.

While it's not your job to find your husband, you can still pray that God leads you to him. You can ask God to choose a godly husband for you and to lead you to this special man in His perfect timing.

You can also look cute (this isn't a crime). I'm amazed at how God speaks of the Proverbs 31 woman as being someone who dresses in "fine linen" (verse 22). You can take care of yourself, brush your hair, wear modest and fashionable outfits (in other words, that fine linen), and ultimately show up as the best version of yourself until your special man comes along and finds you.

Become a Proverbs 31 Woman as You Wait for Your Man of God

You might be confused about what a Proverbs 31 woman is. In Proverbs 31, King Solomon describes the qualities of a godly wife. But you don't need a husband to become this type of woman. You can become her right now.

You can become a woman who wakes up early—even before sunrise. You can become a woman who puts God first in her day through prayer and Bible study, developing a heart that fears and trusts the Lord.

You can become a woman who works hard and is never lazy. You can become a woman who uses her gifts and doesn't let them go to waste. You can even develop a hobby or craft that can provide for your future husband.

You can become a woman who gives to those in need (family, charity) without seeking any validation. You can volunteer in your community and be a blessing to those around you.

You can become a woman who is a good steward of her home. You can love the family God has given you now while you wait for Him to bring you into a new family.

You can become a woman who shows up every day in her best dress and takes care of herself. A woman who clothes herself in dignity, like the royalty that she is. You can still make time for self-care. You *are* royalty, not because you have a ring on your finger, but because you are a daughter of the King.

You can become a woman who is strong and respectable. You can exercise and stay in good health. You can learn how to cook healthy recipes for yourself that will bless your future man (hello, steak, anyone?).

You can become a woman who doesn't fear the future but has her full trust in the Lord.

You can become a woman of love and kindness who speaks with wisdom and gentleness. You can become a woman with incredible character.

You can fully become this Proverbs 31 woman so that when your future husband finds you, he has surely found a good thing.

If You're Fed Up with Your Singleness

You might be like me, still waiting for God to bring your man into your life. You might be questioning Him: "God, do You really know what You're doing?"

It's the most difficult thing in the world to give up control and to trust God in this area—to really wait on His timing. Waiting on God can be a super painful area of our lives—and I want to acknowledge that.

Maybe you've turned down some incredible guys who love Jesus, and it's just because you know, in your heart and soul, that this person isn't your man. I've wrestled with God over this too. I feel like I've been through it all—I've had long periods of time without getting asked out on a single date; I've fallen for the wrong guys; I've had great guys who were interested in me and who loved Jesus, but it just didn't feel right, and I didn't want to force it.

I would be lying to you if I said that there weren't still some really hard moments and that it hasn't been extremely difficult to trust God to write my love story—especially when I feel like I keep getting older and I don't see this man anywhere.

It's especially difficult to believe that I shouldn't try to control or make something happen with my love story but should rather trust that God is going to bring this man—and fulfill this promise—in His perfect timing.

Sometimes I'm tempted to spiral and wonder if marriage is even in God's plan for my life. But then I have to remind myself that the enemy tries to sow doubt in my heart because he knows just how powerful my faith really is.

I had to come out of agreement with those lies and instead begin to declare God's promises over my life.

One scripture I always go back to is Psalm 37:4: "Delight yourself in the LORD, and he will give you the desires of your heart" (ESV).

If I've been delighting myself in the Lord—and the desire to be a wifey and to love a man of God and to start a family legacy with this man hasn't gone away—then I must believe that He will provide for that desire.

Because if it wasn't in His plan for me, He would be so kind to take away that desire as I delight in Him.

What I love about this scripture is that it says, "*He will give you* the desires of your heart." God is the one to give us the gifts that He wants us to receive. It's not on us to strive to make them happen.

The Bible tells us that every good gift comes from above (James 1:17). And it's nothing that can be earned—it's given out of sheer grace and God's love for us.

So if my husband isn't in my life right now, it's because God believes it's not time yet. But in His perfect timing, He will make it happen. And He isn't withholding any good thing from me (Psalm 84:11).

If you've been delighting yourself in the Lord and you also haven't stopped longing for a husband who loves the Lord, it's just not yet the right time. But when it is, God will make it happen. And He isn't withholding any good thing from you.

So, if you are tempted to fall into doubt and hopelessness in this area of your life—this is your reminder to not let the enemy steal your faith.

It's your reminder to keep believing.

And to know that we serve a God of miracles.

God might have this man for you, but it just might not be right now.

Don't Let Your Impatience Abort the Promise

I think of Sarah and Abraham, who the Bible tells us were given a promise from God. They were both in their old age when God told them that they would have a child and would birth an entire nation (Genesis 12:1–3).

The only issue is that Sarah, Abe's wife, was completely barren. She had been to countless baby showers at this point and probably was way past the point of believing it could happen for her.

She got tired of waiting, and I don't blame her. In her impatience, seeing no action from God in this area of her life, she took matters into her own hands. She told her husband to sleep with her servant, Hagar, hoping to have children through her servant, thinking she was too old to have them herself (16:1–2).

This was a big issue, as you can imagine, because this wasn't God's will for their lives. You see, there is free will and there is God's will. We can choose.

Although the Bible doesn't clearly say that Sarah's disobedience delayed the promise, I wonder if her decision to take matters into her own hands made her have to wait another fourteen years to have a child of her own. Furthermore, the descendants of the child born to Hagar (Ishmael) and Sarah's own child (Isaac) experienced conflict (25:18). This strife has continued in the enduring division between the Muslim and Jewish populations today.

This one mistake created a ripple effect of brokenness

through the generations, all because Sarah wasn't willing to be faithful and patient by waiting on God's timing.

God is a good, kind God. I think of Abraham, who the Bible tells us was given a promise from God. He was in his old age when God told him that he would have a child and would be the father of an entire nation (Genesis 12:1–3).

I love how *The Message* version of the Bible describes the redemption of this story:

> Abraham and Sarah were old by this time, very old. Sarah was far past the age for having babies. Sarah laughed within herself, "An old woman like me? Get pregnant? With this old man of a husband?"
>
> GOD said to Abraham, "Why did Sarah laugh saying, 'Me? Have a baby? An old woman like me?' Is anything too hard for GOD? I'll be back about this time next year and Sarah will have a baby." (18:11–14)

And what do you know? At just the time God said, Sarah was pregnant:

> The LORD kept his word and did for Sarah exactly what he had promised. She became pregnant, and she gave birth to a son for Abraham in his old age. This happened at just the time God had said it would. (21:1–2, NLT)

This story reminds me that I can never do something better than God can. And when my faith is under attack and I'm tempted to doubt God's ability, I become susceptible to taking matters into my own hands, especially in relationships.

I'm vulnerable to going on every dating app under the sun.

I'm vulnerable to scanning rooms at church or Bible studies to see if any cute guys are around.

I'm vulnerable to settling for the guy that I know deep down isn't the man God put in my heart as my future husband—but at least it would be convenient, and at least I would finally have a ring on my finger.

If you're like me, during this time of waiting, it's easy to feel completely out of control. But as we've talked about, there are still some decisions you have control over and things you can do while you wait. You can be faithful to God as you wait for Him to bring a man into your life:

- Pray for this man and ask the Lord to lead you to him. You can pray that God would make it obvious to this man that you are to be his wife, so much so that you won't have to be the one to make it happen.
- Look at the areas God has given you to steward in this season of life, instead of burying your gifts in the ground. You can make the most of where you are now, knowing that God has you in this season for a reason. And as you are faithful to Him, God will surely be faithful to give you more.
- Wait in patience for the man God has for you—because He is powerful enough to put this man in your life.
- Choose to resist giving in to doubt. You can keep believing, knowing that we serve a God of miracles and, in His perfect timing, He will make things happen.

So let's allow this time to build patient endurance in us, and let's steward what He's given us: the people, the job, our relationship with Him, our other gifts.

We get to believe God is going to make things happen, while making the most of where He has us right now. He will surely not waste a thing.

6

Planting for the Future

BEING FAITHFUL IN WORK

Ever since I wrote my very first story in first grade, I dreamed of a career as an author. You would think that this dream would have been less and less exciting as I grew older, but the ambition only grew. During my final year of college, I applied for many jobs, but I knew that none of them would bring me the peace or excitement that the thought of becoming an author did. Why, after all these years, couldn't I imagine myself doing anything else?

After graduating from college, I found myself back in my childhood home in a suburb in Ohio. Many of my closest college friends were moving forward with their lives, applying the degrees they had just earned and settling into their post-grad apartments.

And as for me? I stayed home with my mom—with my dream to become an author.

A lot of people doubted the wisdom of my decision to stay home and pursue a pipe dream. Many said I wouldn't ever make any money writing books. My mother, on the other hand, was so kind to let me stay with her instead of urging me to go down the conventional route of getting a nine-to-five job, and her generosity was truly a godsend. Being a big dreamer and entrepreneur herself, she understood that to chase after big dreams, you need support.

Alongside writing, another dream grew in my heart, a dream to develop an online ministry. I graduated from college in 2020, the year Instagram reels were born. I felt God lead me to start making videos and posting consistently on social media to encourage people through a screen.

While my friends were getting real-world jobs and living in their cool downtown apartments, I was creating videos that only a couple hundred people would see. I could have felt that I was regressing in life. But oddly enough, I had such peace—peace that carried me until I saw breakthrough.

Five years have passed since I made that decision to go all in with the dreams God gave me. Since then, He has helped me build an online audience of hundreds of thousands, establish an online business, produce a docuseries, and author several books.

And if I hadn't taken that leap of faith to pursue those dreams God put on my heart, who knows if I would be writing this book to you today?

God Gives You a Dream for a Reason

Isn't it interesting that we don't all have the same dream?

One of my best friends has a dream to worship Jesus on stages around the world and to write songs that bring people closer to God. Another friend wants to pursue justice in the human trafficking space, assisting girls who have gone through the worst of the worst. And another friend aspires to create street-style clothing that glorifies God.

You'll notice that none of these friends have the same dream. And I believe that's because a very kind God is guiding each of the dreams on our hearts.

Take a moment to consider your dreams, no matter how crazy they seem. Consider if you are taking any steps of faith to pursue them. You might feel convicted, believing you are sitting on dreams that God told you to move on. I want to encourage you to believe our faithful God could make those dreams happen for you. I would hate for you to go your whole life not pursuing your God-given dreams out of fear that they might be unattainable.

Sure, pursuing those dreams and a life of faith isn't always easy. In fact, I would argue that it's the tougher route than the worldly course most take. I could have chosen the predictable path, one I wasn't too crazy about. Had I chosen to follow the crowd and ignored that still, small voice telling me to go another route, I would have missed out on the incredible things God is doing in my life right now. You, too, have the choice either to take the easy route or to follow the path

God has laid out for you, where you pursue the dreams He has placed on your heart.

If You're Not Seeing the Fruit of Your Labor

In the early post-grad days of living with my mom, I had around five thousand followers on Instagram. Sitting at the kitchen table in my childhood home late at night, I would engage on my platform, responding to people's comments and dreaming up new content to post.

Each morning, I'd wake up expecting crazy growth, only to find my account barely grew at all. But I was determined not to give up. Days of diligently managing the platform God gave me turned into weeks, and weeks turned into months. Months turned into years of consistently showing up to create videos and engage with an audience. Through diligence and consistency, that modest Instagram account of five thousand followers eventually grew into a thriving community of more than six hundred thousand.

I didn't realize until later that the process I went through is a business concept called *building momentum*.[1] Momentum is a sustained, positive force that helps a company move toward its goals.

At first, the process of building momentum may look grim and bleak—like the stagnant number of followers I had for quite some time. You are trying to move something that was once at a standstill, and it requires all your effort to get it going. You just need to take one small step, one action at a time. Progress can feel slow, maybe even hopeless, as you wonder when things will accelerate on their own.

But then, as new habits are formed and consistency is maintained, momentum starts to build. That's when you begin to see results in that very area.

Galatians 6:9 says, "Let us not become weary in doing good, for at the proper time we will reap a harvest if we do not give up." Even God knew that, at the beginning of building momentum, we might grow weary. Building something from the ground up can be exhausting. It can feel like the dream is always out of reach, almost impossible to achieve.

But if you persist and you show up every day, you'll eventually reap a harvest of blessings and see the fruit of your labor.

How to Build Momentum

Perhaps you, too, have a big dream—one you even feel God has given you. Likely, there are days when you diligently nurture that dream, only to fall off the next day, making the dream feel so far away.

The way to ultimately see the harvest you want is to build momentum. In a nutshell, here's the process:

1. Make new choices based on the dream God has given you.
2. Let those choices bring about new behaviors.
3. Repeat those actions long enough to establish new habits.
4. Build those habits into your daily routines.
5. Stay consistent long enough to see the harvest.

Many successful people do the same things before *and* after they see momentum. They faithfully cultivate habits, routines, and consistency in their lives long enough to finally unlock momentum.

Often it's not about whether something is possible but rather about your willingness to stay faithful long enough for God to bring a breakthrough.

Start with a Vision

Many people question their purpose: what path God wants them to follow, like what they should major in or what job they should take. In my case, I questioned many times if being an author was really in God's plan for me, because so often it seemed unlikely that it would actually happen. To keep going, I had to establish a clear vision.

We wonder why we don't feel motivated—why doing our schoolwork feels like such a drag or why we struggle every day to go to work. I think the answer often lies in the fact that our vision is foggy. Our vision isn't strong enough to keep us motivated through the challenges we face in our work. Proverbs 29:18 says, "Where there is no vision, the people perish: but he that keepeth the law, happy is he" (KJV). Clearly, vision is crucial.

If you want to get fresh vision on what God wants you to do, you must spend time alone with Him. Sometimes that alone time might feel like you're in a wilderness season. In a wilderness season, God might reveal your weaknesses, point out poor habits, and get you ready for new opportunities.

Although it can be uncomfortable, it's a chance to strengthen your faith, learn to rely on Him, and be transformed. It's a time to listen to God and gain direction from Him.

In the Bible, we see countless times when God put His people in a wilderness season. The greatest example was when Jesus was alone in the wilderness, praying and fasting before He began His mission. The Israelites had their own wilderness season when they eventually heard God's word and moved forward in faith. For these people, that period in isolation may have felt like a dark time but it gave them an opportunity to hear from God.

I learned recently that the Hebrew word for "wilderness" comes from the root word for "to speak."[2] This means that, in the wilderness season, you get to hear the voice of God. So, to get fresh vision from God and to really know what He wants you to do, you must find time to get alone with Him and listen for His voice.

What Is a Vision from God?

A vision is an inspiring mental picture that propels us to take action. When it comes to getting a vision from God, it's getting a picture of what's possible with Him. He will give us a vision to prompt us to be obedient to the call on our lives. It can even come at what seems to be the most random time.

Three years ago, I was dog sitting for my dad for a weekend. It was just me and his dog in his house, no other friends or family. I felt God tell me that I needed to be alone all weekend, listening to His voice. This happened during a time when I was at a crossroads—feeling like I needed to be doing something else in my ministry, but I wasn't sure what that was.

Alone in that house, I saw an opportunity to seek fresh direction from God. I asked Him to speak to me. Then I listened. I dreamed with God. I journaled what I felt He was putting on my heart.

And at the end of the weekend, I was sure of what He was asking me to do.

The clear vision I received inspired me to begin to take action—small steps in the right direction—that has resulted in where I am today.

When you have a clear vision from God, you will have clear focus. The more focus you have, the more chance you will take action. And it's very likely that if the vision is from God, He will bless those steps of faith you take to see His vision come true.

How to Get a Vision from God

Seek vision from God by asking Him to provide it. It's that simple. Get alone with Him and ask Him to tell you how He sees you as His daughter. Speak with Him and quiet your thoughts enough to hear His voice in return.

When I've asked God for vision in the past, it wasn't like I immediately heard His voice in my right ear or saw my next action steps written in the clouds in the sky. Sometimes it has taken weeks of diligent prayer and fasting to get clarity on what God is asking me to do. But as I continue to seek what He is inviting me into, the vision eventually comes.

You might think this would be a good time to create a vision board. My problem with vision boards is that they teach us to look inward—for self to be the guide. Instead of creating a vision board, I craft a prayer board. This is where I ask God to solidify His vision for my life. I write down the goals He puts on my heart, the visions He gives me, and the action steps I feel He is leading me to take. I look at this prayer board often to solidify my focus and to remind me of what God said, especially when I'm tempted to stray from my routines or fall into doubt.

One thing that helps clear my mind and allows me to hear God more is fasting. Starting the year with a fast, whether it's a Daniel Fast (basically becoming vegan for three weeks and giving up caffeine and alcohol), a partial fast (omitting sweets and dairy), or even a no-food fast from sunup to sundown, can be a meaningful way to seek clarity and vision from God.

We can make our plans, but God determines how we get there. He charts the course. Over the years, God has given me visions and then guided me creatively to achieve those goals, often in unexpected ways and not always according to my timeline. Yet I trust that if He has given me the vision, He will provide the resources and strategies needed to fulfill it.

Is This Vision from God or from Me?

You might wonder, *How do I know if a vision is from God? How can I tell the difference between dreams from God and those that are from the flesh?*

To know if a vision is from God, we must begin with hearts of surrender, wanting to do His will above anything else. That's where fasting and prayer come in, where we are emptying ourselves and being filled with His Spirit to hear how we can be most obedient to His plan.

We must begin with hearts of surrender—but this next part is crucial. After we surrender, we must trust that the vision on our hearts is from Him. And we can trust that it's from Him because we started in a posture of wanting to receive guidance from Him and Him alone.

Isn't it interesting that if a group of people all choose to fast and pray together at the beginning of the year, at the end of the fast each person will come out with different visions? Or different things that God spoke over them to do? Psalm 37:4 says, "Delight yourself in the LORD, and he will give you the desires of your heart" (ESV). It's easy to doubt whether the desires God puts on your heart are in fact from Him. But I'd argue that if those desires have come after you surrendered everything to the Lord and if those desires align with His, then they are from Him.

Whether it's leading worship, traveling to Africa as a missionary, becoming a teacher, starting to homeschool your children, or getting married—whatever the vision may be—if you've surrendered everything to God, if your desire aligns with His Word and brings you peace, and if the vision persists, I believe it's from God.

Choose to trust the vision He has given you, and take steps of obedience in that direction. By taking action, you show your belief in what God has spoken to you. He isn't going to be upset with your actions taken in faith. And if by any chance you got it wrong, He will reroute you onto the right path.

Over the past four years, I've achieved at least five goals from my yearly list. This is not because I'm special but because I've made space to listen to God's voice and follow His guidance. It truly is proof of Proverbs 16:3: "Roll your works upon the Lord [commit and trust them wholly to Him; He will cause your thoughts to become agreeable to His will, and] so shall your plans be established *and* succeed" (AMPC).

Reaching my goals was possible by following these same steps, year after year:

- At the start of each year, seek God's visions for my life and surrender my plans for the year to Him.
- Write down the visions He gives me.
- Commit to the process of reaching those visions by taking action each week.
- See Him bless my obedience.

Vision helps you take action. So, if you find yourself struggling to take action, I suggest questioning how strong your vision is. Don't underestimate the power of seeking wisdom from the Lord and getting quiet enough to hear His voice. He wants to guide you. And He will always speak into a heart that is willing to receive from Him.

How to Know What God Wants You to Do

You might still feel uncertain about how to know for sure if a dream on your heart is from God or if it's from your flesh. You can wonder what God is saying about which career path you should go down, who you should marry, or which church you should go to.

I used to struggle with this concept a lot. The problem was that I was getting visions and messages from God but my doubts were holding me back, making me question if what I was hearing was really from Him. Because of my doubts, I wasn't moving forward in faith.

Then I listened to a podcast with Jamie Winship, and it was life-changing. It's all about discovering your God-given identity and hearing God's voice. He very simply describes hearing from God as "the free flow of thoughts that go through your mind when you fix your eyes on Jesus and ask Him a question."[3]

You might be wondering, *Well, what do I even ask God?* It might be tempting to ask Him "Why?" But God isn't always going to tell us why something is happening. He asks us to trust Him, instead of trying to understand what's going on (Proverbs 3:5–6). Winship shifts us from asking "Why?" to asking these two simple questions:

1. God, what do You want me to know?
2. God, what do You want me to do?[4]

When I heard this, it gave me so much peace. It took away my need to always get it right and led me to instead trust that what God put in my mind after I asked Him these two questions truly was from Him. I also noted how many times in Scripture people would commune with God as if He were their friend—like how Moses spoke to God face-to-face (Exodus 33:11) and Abraham was called a friend of God (Isaiah 41:8).

With this understanding, I realized that, through the Holy Spirit and because of Jesus's death on the cross, I could also talk to God as if He were my best friend. I could discern what He has to say to me and the guidance He wants to speak into my life.

I could ask Him about my career. I could ask Him about who to date. I could ask Him if I should have coffee or matcha. He is my friend, and He cares about every little decision I have to make. I had to realize that I could very simply just ask Him what I wanted to know. And He very simply would tell me what He thought.

With my eyes fixed on Jesus, I start in a place of surrender, emptying myself and asking God to lead me on His perfect path for my life. I share with Him what's on my heart, and I tell Him the truth of what's really going on. Then I ask Him a very simple question: "God, what do You want me to know about this?" Or, "God, what do You want me to do?" And then I pay attention to the thoughts that go freely through my mind as I fix my eyes on Jesus. And in that, I can trust that whatever I'm hearing, I'm hearing from God. I get to then change my thinking on the situation and be transformed from the inside out.

You might be wondering, *But what if that's your* own *will, Ashley? What if you're just hearing your own thoughts?*

And to that I would say, "Am I asking myself these questions and listening to my own heart? No. I'm beginning in a posture of surrender and wanting to hear from God alone. I'm emptying myself and taking myself out of the equation. And I'm diligently asking God and allowing Him to speak."

It's truly that simple.

God wants to speak to you. He wants to have intimate friendship with you. He wants to guide you in every decision you need to make, even if it seems like it's little or even if it's big.

Satan wants to make hearing from your heavenly Father complicated. God wants to make it simple. He is your friend—and isn't it so very simple to speak with a friend?

If You're Focused on Everything, You're Focused on Nothing

God rarely asks me to do a million things at once. He normally gives me a vision followed by a specific action He wants me to undertake. When I look at Scripture, I see similar examples. When God saw the suffering of the slaves in Egypt, He wanted to rescue them from the Egyptians, so He told Moses, "Now go to the king! I am sending you to lead my people out of his country" (Exodus 3:10, CEV). When God revealed to Abraham that he would be a father of many nations (meaning he would have many descendants), He simply told him, "Go from your country, your people and your father's household to the land I will show you" (Genesis 12:1).

God started out by showing these biblical heroes a vision. And then He gave an action step to take to move forward in that very direction.

God knows how limited we are. He knows that in order for things to change, we must be committed to seeing a difference and not be pulled in a million directions at once. Satan will try to distract you with a ton of priorities so you will feel overwhelmed and make no effective change anywhere. But God, on the other hand, will show you specifically what He wants you to focus on so progress can be made in that area. He knows that if everything is a focus, nothing is a focus.

If you put a piece of paper on the ground on a summer day, nothing changes. But if you put a magnifying glass between a piece of paper and the sun and the glass focuses the sunlight, the paper will eventually catch on fire. Similarly, when God gives you a clear vision and clear direction, you must be disciplined to focus on that one thing if you want to see results. You must let go of the things that are of lesser importance. You must decide what you are *not* going to do so you can instead focus on what God told you to do.

On any given day, many distractions will arise, tempting you to take your eyes off what's most important. And the enemy will try everything in his power to distract you from the mission and vision God is leading you toward.

To minimize distraction, I define my priorities at the beginning of the month, week, and day. I ensure these priorities are set before I schedule anything else or respond to requests from other people. When I put the processes it takes to achieve my priorities in my calendar first, I ensure my time is dedicated to what is most important, rather than falling into the temptation to fill my time with what is urgent but less important.

If you are going to focus on what God is telling you to do, you must be diligent to say no to many things. To maintain focus on my work, I have to avoid answering the phone and sometimes even delay responding until the afternoon, once my tasks are completed. I also have to be diligent to decline some meetups or even cool and exciting opportunities that would divert my attention from something that is more important.

Every yes you say is a no to something else. Saying yes to

everything is something I've had to work on in the past, and I still do. But then I remind myself that distractions are the enemy's way of diverting me from my true priorities.

Change What You Think About When You Think About Yourself

Several biblical heroes experienced doubt when God spoke to them about their calling. Both Moses and Gideon questioned whether they were the right men for the missions God was calling them to.

As with Moses and Gideon, God chose you for your tasks and will be with you as you do them (Exodus 3–4; Judges 6).

Because here's the truth: If you weren't the person God chose for a particular mission, He simply wouldn't have called you to do it. If God is calling you to do something and if He is giving you a vision for it, you are the person for the job. And He often calls the ones who seem the least likely or the least qualified.

We see this throughout history. William Seymour, who was born to formerly enslaved parents and had only one eye, became the leader of the Azusa Street Revival in Los Angeles. Despite his challenges, Seymour was called by God to start a revival in Southern California, bringing Black, White, Asian, and Hispanic people together at a time when such unity was unheard of.

Abraham Lincoln grew up in poverty in Kentucky and Indiana, lost his mother when he was just nine years old, and lost two of his sons before they reached adulthood. Despite his life of hardship and sorrow, God called him to be the president of the United States, leading our country to abolish the evil of slavery and to free millions of enslaved people in the States.

Rahab was a prostitute. David had an affair. Noah got drunk. Peter had a temper. Sarah was impatient. Moses had a stutter. Paul persecuted Christians. Yet God called each of them to a specific assignment. God doesn't call the qualified; He qualifies the called.

Several times in Scripture, when God gave one of His people a vision, He told them that they were the person for the mission. He spoke over them their true identity, even if they didn't believe it themselves.

Although Abraham was very old and uncertain about the future of his wealth, God spoke to him, changing his name from Abram to Abraham, which means "father of a multitude,"[5] and promising that he would become "the father of many nations" (Genesis 17:3).

Sarah was too old to bear children and was losing hope that she would ever have a natural conception. But God promised, "She will be the mother of nations; kings of peoples will come from her" (verse 16). He told Abraham, her hubby, to stop calling her Sarai but to instead call her Sarah, which means "princess" or "a woman of high rank."[6]

Peter denied Jesus three times when He went to the cross, saying that he never had a relationship with Him. But Jesus told Peter, "You are Peter, and on this rock I will build my church" (Matthew 16:18).

God told people who they were, even if they didn't see themselves in the same light. And these people were brave enough to believe Him. Because they believed who God said they were and what they were capable of, it changed their attitude about themselves and about the God they served. And that attitude prompted them to take action. That action then yielded powerful results.

If God has given you a vision for which you don't feel equipped, ask Him to tell you why He chose you and what He sees in you that will allow you to bring this task life. Let Him show you why you are the person for the job.

The Power of Routine

Consistent daily practices are key to success in any area of life. We must establish a routine we can commit to. The more difficult the goal we want to achieve, the more diligent we must be about sticking with our routine.

Consistency is hard. Discipline is difficult. Many people are unwilling to show up every day to achieve the life they desire. But for your God-given dream to come to fruition, you must be faithful to show up and be obedient, even when you don't want to—a principle we covered earlier. You must pre-decide your commitment.

I love this quote when it comes to committing to what God has called you to do: "Commitment is doing the thing you said you were going to do long after the mood you said it in has left you."[7] In order to accomplish beautiful things with God, we must commit to them no matter how we feel.

Consider the dream God has given you. The goal He wants you to pursue. Then ask Him what daily and weekly rhythms will enable you to be faithful with this dream.

Let's put it practically. If you want to be a songwriter and singer, how often will you show up to write music? If you want to be an author, how often will you show up to write your manuscript? If you want to be a podcaster, how often will you show up to record? Pre-decide what you will do to sow in this area of your life. Write out your routine somewhere you can see it every day. And over time, your faithfulness will pay off.

Make It Realistic

Last year, I made an audacious goal of posting at least seven times a day on TikTok. That was a little crazy, but I set out to do it. Only, I couldn't stick with this new routine of writing all this content and recording it in a day without being completely exhausted by the end of every single week. I failed to create a sustainable routine, which was necessary to prevent the cycle of starting and stopping repeatedly.

Because I had started to build and train a team at this point, I was also letting my team in on the new goal. We were going strong in that rhythm for a few months, but it got to a point where we were all absolutely exhausted. We needed to scale our content production back if we wanted to remain consistent.

This same thing happens with exercise goals. I have a friend who really wanted to get into working out this year. For a long time, she was mostly inactive. At the beginning of the year, we devised a simple workout plan for her, where she would exercise three times a week and work her way up from there.

She then began to add on to this new routine out of pure excitement and vigor. Instead of working out three times a week, she made a goal to work out every single day. She would wake up at seven in the morning—a full two hours earlier than usual. After spending an hour with God first thing, she would be off to the gym.

You can imagine how this went.

Because she went from zero to one hundred, she couldn't be consistent with any of it. She didn't even start.

What she needed was a more sustainable schedule. She needed to start slow and start small, because small steps eventually lead to big change.

You don't want to be that person who makes such crazy goals for themselves that they show up strong one week and then drop off the next. It's okay if you go hard for a while, but you need to build a routine you can consistently come back to.

Here's the simple breakdown of the process:

1. Decide the goal you want to pursue.
2. Determine the routine you need to establish to achieve growth in this area. Make sure this new routine is something you can be consistent with.
3. Write it on your calendar, whether that's your daily, weekly, or monthly calendar. Put it somewhere you can see every single day.

Consistency is a critical element of success.

How to Schedule Your Days

When God really wants me to get something done, I will be disciplined to see it to the finish line. One of the ways I do that is by being very specific about how I schedule my days and weeks and months.

As I mentioned earlier in this chapter, at the beginning of each year, I fast and ask God what He wants me to do for that year. Then after about a month of seeking Him and His will, I feel Him reveal what it is He is asking me to pursue that year. I write these goals down and put them on my prayer board, where I can see them every day.

At the beginning of each month, I ask God what He wants me to focus on for the month that will move me toward the goals He gave me for the year. The goals can be pursued in different seasons and in different orders, but I listen for the Holy Spirit's direction for that month. It may be influenced by other activities, what the Spirit reveals when I pray, and even where I find the most peace as I move forward. Then I write only three goals to focus on for the month, and I place them where I can see them every day.

At the beginning of each week, I look at the month's three goals and consider what I can be doing this week to make progress on them. I write down what I feel God is leading me to do for that week and schedule it.

At the beginning of each day, I look at my list for the week and consider what the top three things are that I can get done that day to make progress on my goals for the week. Then I get those top three most important tasks done first. After that, I will focus on the rest of my to-do list, which includes things that need to be done but aren't as urgent.

We Don't Accomplish Goals by Focusing on Them

If you want a certain outcome, you must commit yourself to a process that will achieve that desired outcome. In his book *The Power to Change,* Craig Groeschel writes, "Obsess over the process instead of the outcome. You don't get results by focusing on results. You get results by focusing on the actions that get results."[8] In other words, you don't reach a goal by obsessing over your goal every single day. You reach it by obsessing over the process needed to get to that goal. James Clear says it this way in *Atomic Habits:* "You do not rise to the level of your goals. You fall to the level of your systems."[9]

You can't always control when you will hit a certain goal. You can't control the competition. You can't control the economy. You can't control the circumstances that are going on around you.

But you can control being consistent and faithful. You can choose to have a positive outlook. You can choose to follow God and stay committed to what He put on your heart to do.

I have a friend who struggled to make time to cook. Feeling lazy, she would often eat only two meals. This left her with little energy, creating a vicious cycle of doing it all over again the next day.

To keep this from happening, she made it a goal this year

to take care of herself by eating three meals each day. But she quickly found herself discouraged after failing to meet her goal day after day.

What she needed to do was to fall in love with the process of having three solid meals a day. She needed to fall in love with making a weekly meal plan, going to the grocery store, as well as cooking every day. If she put these processes into place, over time she would reach her goal of eating three whole daily meals and have an abundance of energy because of it.

No matter what your vision is, you must embrace the journey to get there. Focus on falling in love with the *process*, not the goal. When you engage in the process week after week, your dedication will lead to the desired outcome.

Don't Forget the Power of Rest

After Monday through Friday early mornings, hard work, and gym workouts each week, it's time for some much-needed rest.

Every Saturday, I have a day off that is my Sabbath. This is a day when I don't go on social media, I don't run errands, and instead, I focus on rest, rejuvenation, and God. I make sure I sleep in as long as my body needs, then start my day with time with Jesus.

Every Sabbath feels wonderful like Christmas morning, as sometimes I stay in my jammies all morning.

On my cherished day off, I love to journal, pray, and review my goals.

This is definitely a time to indulge in my favorite takeout instead of cooking, as I've cooked my meals all week. I usually treat myself to a latte or matcha. In the evening, I like to see friends who are peaceful and relaxing to be around.

Whenever I need a reminder to rest, I reflect on Genesis 2:2–3:

> By the seventh day God had finished the work he had been doing; so on the seventh day he rested from all his work. Then God blessed the seventh day and made it holy, because on it he rested from all the work of creating that he had done.

If we are made in God's image and He chose to rest, what makes us think that we shouldn't prioritize rest?

It's not always easy to rest. There is always something on our to-do list because we get to the end of the week and still have things left over to accomplish.

It can be so tempting to not take a rest day seriously. But we must. The Bible underscores the importance of a rest day—and so does science. Research suggests that "rest is vital for good mental health, increased concentration and memory, a healthier immune system, reduced stress, improved mood and even a better metabolism."[10]

Taking a day off each week to disconnect from work and limit phone use, instead focusing on rest, reflection, and relaxation with God, can do wonders for both your physical and your mental health. It can also help you grow closer to God.

God Will Promote You

You might feel like your work will never pay off. Maybe you've been in a season when you consistently show up day after day yet it feels like no one notices or appreciates your work.

Maybe you've been working hard for a very long time, only to see others who started after you seem to be light-years ahead of you. It can be discouraging when we keep showing up every day but we feel like we'll never see a breakthrough. These are the times it's tempting to compare ourselves with others, aspiring to be someone we're not, or try to get a promotion for ourselves.

Whenever I feel this way, I find comfort in the story of Daniel (Daniel 1–2). As a young man, Daniel was taken captive by the Babylonians and selected to serve in the court of King Nebuchadnezzar. For three years, Daniel and a group of other young men trained in literature and language to prepare for service in the king's palace.

But Daniel was set apart from this group, just by the way he lived. He and three of his friends chose not to eat the king's food or drink his wine, because this was against Jewish law. Instead, they chose to be on a different diet of only vegetables.

Daniel also had a God-given ability to interpret visions and dreams. Eventually, the king had a dream and demanded not only that his astrologers and enchanters tell him what he had seen in his dream but also interpret its meaning. None of them were able to, but after Daniel told the king the dream and interpreted it correctly, he was promoted and made ruler of the whole province of Babylon.

The reason Daniel was distinguished in this way is that "an excellent spirit was in him" (Daniel 6:3, ESV). And he was faithful. Daniel didn't get to the next level by seeking the promotion—it was his faithfulness and spirit that eventually earned him the king's favor.

Perhaps you've heard that "success occurs when opportunity meets preparation."[11] In Scripture, we see this in action. Daniel worked hard and was faithful, and he lived a life that honored God.

Because Daniel was ready when the opportunity came for him to interpret the dream, he earned a high position in the king's court. In effect, he was made rich and famous overnight. His faithfulness led him to be promoted again and again.

When the opportunity came for him to show the excellent spirit that was in him in front of the king, he was ready. And because of that, he achieved success.

Live with an Excellent Spirit

An excellent spirit, like Daniel's, involves doing things well, being faithful to God, and having a desire to bring glory to Him. It's "the quality of being outstanding or extremely good."[12]

An excellent spirit includes these characteristics:

Faithfulness: being loyal to God and committed to what He calls you to do

Diligence: doing things with excellence

Organization: being orderly
Planning: preparing for the future
Determination: not giving up when things get tough
Stewardship: taking proper care of what has been entrusted to you
Integrity: living up to your commitments, even when it's difficult
Discipline: having self-control and making sacrifices and other choices that may not be popular but are ultimately best for you
Full faith in and reliance on God: trusting Him completely and knowing He is in control of all things; relying on God instead of relying on yourself

Some of us aren't being promoted at work because we simply aren't working hard. But God honors our hard work. Daniel, at the end of the day, was a man of work. He carried out his responsibilities with excellence.

Daniel was also a man of discipline. He had no problem disciplining his body by eating only veggies for ten days, while everyone around him was enjoying meat and wine (hence the reason we call it the Daniel Fast). He disciplined his mind by being a diligent student for three years, still standing apart from the rest of his peers. He disciplined himself to pray three times a day to God, even when it was taboo to pray to anyone but the king.

Daniel was also loyal to God. Even being thrown into a lion's den, he stayed loyal. When everyone else was living a life of compromise, he chose to live a life of godliness.

This isn't the only time we see an excellent spirit in the

Bible. After Joseph was sold as a slave, he was entrusted with authority over his master's household. Eventually, Joseph's excellence and faithfulness led him to be the second most powerful person in all of Egypt (Genesis 39–41).

If you are feeling like you will never reach a breakthrough in your work, I want you to take a page out of the book of Daniel and look to see if these qualities are at work in your life:

You are loyal to God, above all else, and are led by His Spirit.
You are faithful to the God-given assignment.
You are diligent and do everything you've been given to do.
You are organized and prepared for the future.
You are determined to do everything with excellence, even when it's inconvenient.
You take proper care of what God has put in your hands today.
You live with integrity, are honest, and carry purity of heart.
You live a disciplined lifestyle.
You have insurmountable faith—believing that God is able and that the Spirit is greater than any power in the world, even if you were being thrown into a lion's den.

When I'm tempted to compare myself with others—or to be discouraged because I'm not as far along as I'd like to be—I have to remind myself to control what I can control. I have to remind myself of Daniel's story, where he was focused on being faithful and living with an excellent spirit. I have to remember that, at the right time, God brought him to his promotion and He will do the same for His people.

If you live with faithfulness and diligence, honoring God, eventually opportunity will come to you.

Having an excellent spirit will *always* produce fruit. Remember to focus less on getting the promotion and put more of your effort into being faithful. Your faithfulness will eventually lead to fruitfulness.

God Wants You to Be Fruitful in Your Work

When you give your life to the Lord, He will commission you. In other words, He will send you out on a mission.

If you aren't seeing a breakthrough in your life, turn to the Lord today and seek His guidance. Seek God for a vision only He can give you. Then ask Him for the process to get there. Get counsel from the people He leads you to.

Once you can discern the process, commit to consistently showing up and being faithful to that process. Over time, your consistency will compound, and you will eventually reap the harvest of all the seeds you've so diligently sown. Let the planting process begin.

7

Eating Well, Moving More, Sleeping Soundly

BEING FAITHFUL IN HEALTH

I remember the first time I felt self-conscious about my body. I was in college, and I looked down at the number on the scale I stood on. I felt shame and guilt because I wasn't the same weight as my sixteen-year-old self. In that moment, I didn't have compassion for my body and how it was developing as I grew older. Instead, I expected myself to be as skinny as I was growing up. And this is what led me into an unhealthy relationship with food and exercise.

It was around the same time as my breakup and my parents' divorce. With everything feeling out of control, I began clinging to something I could control. And I could control what I ate. By not eating enough, I could look the way I did in high school.

I lost a lot of weight in that season. And honestly, felt great about it. But the constant thought of needing to eat less, needing to work out more, needing to change my body—it left me feeling empty. It wasn't sustainable, and no matter how much I tried to control my weight, it would never be enough.

It's been years since that season. And I'll be honest: There are still days and moments when I'm tempted to revert to the girl who was obsessed with food and exercise. And I have to diligently take my thoughts captive to not make this area of my life an idol.

At the same time, the Lord has given me such a passion for wellness, nutrition, and movement. Now so many people ask me how to start eating healthy and actually enjoy it. Others ask how to start a workout routine. And many ask how you can incorporate God into both of these things. This is living proof of God's redemption in my story when I gave up control and trusted Him.

In this chapter, we are going to cover how we can love and honor God with the way we take care of our bodies. Not shaming our bodies, not making our bodies an idol, and not neglecting our bodies, as some may be in the habit of doing.

But instead, we are going to worship God with this mighty temple He's given us. And to find so much joy and confidence as we do so.

If You Don't Know Where to Start

I literally didn't know how to boil water when I was in college. I'm not kidding. I had to watch a YouTube video on how to do it—that's how bad my knowledge of cooking was. For years, my idea of cooking was preparing packaged foods like Hamburger Helper. I would even go to the extreme of saying how much I *hated* cooking.

I also struggled a lot with emotional eating, turning to the pantry whenever I felt anxious or sad. I would eat in response to any "bad" emotion. I didn't know how to stop, and this would make me feel hopeless.

After years of poor eating habits, I realized I needed to live a healthier lifestyle. I knew I needed to take care of my body as a temple of the Holy Spirit. But making that decision and implementing it are very different things.

One day, to eat healthy, I put together a salad of tomatoes and cucumbers. As I ate it, I thought it was the nastiest meal I'd ever had. I wish I'd had a mentor to walk me through how to eat healthy food and actually enjoy it.

Maybe you can relate to my story. Maybe you struggle to put down the junk food and choose a healthier option instead. Maybe the gym intimidates you, and you really have no idea where to start with moving your body. Or maybe you have a bad habit of starting and stopping workout and healthy eating plans because of a lack of motivation and guidance.

But what I've realized is that taking care of the body God gave you—and not being ashamed of it or neglecting it—is another aspect of being faithful to Him.

On the other hand, if we obsess over what we are (or are not) eating and how much we are (or are not) working out, we can begin to idolize food and exercise, prioritizing our relationship with food and exercise over our relationship with God. Our worth is no longer found in how God views us but in how our bodies look. And this isn't how God wants us to live. He wants us to glorify Him with the way we take care of the bodies He gave us, but it can be so difficult to know how to truly do that.

I'm not a dietician or personal trainer, but God has taught me a few things over the years about how to take care of the body He gave me. In this chapter, we'll cover some of the things I've learned so you can approach this area of your life with confidence. These are the kinds of things I wish someone would have shared with me when I was starting my journey to be faithful in my health.

Let this be a beginner's guide to taking care of your body as a temple of the Holy Spirit and doing it with faithfulness instead of giving up before you see any progress.

You Are So Much More Than Your Weight

Before we get into the nitty-gritty of healthy eating and exercise, we must start off with one truth: You are beautiful, no matter what you look like.

I know that sounds cheesy, but it's a truth we must cling to when we start this journey. A lot of us want to take care of our bodies to feel more confident. And yes, feeling confident might be a by-product of taking care of our bodies for the first time in our lives.

But if we base our self-worth on what we look like, we are in for a rude awakening when life seasons change. When we get pregnant and we literally must put on weight to carry a human inside us and we have to rest instead of running six miles a day.

Or when we get older and wrinkles come and maybe we aren't as ripped as we were in our twenties. It's all okay, and it's all a part of life.

Our confidence can't be found in our stomach size. It can't be based on the number on the scale for the day. Our confidence must be found in Christ.

The Bible talks about how we are "fearfully and wonderfully made" (Psalm 139:14), and this isn't contingent on our weight. You are fearfully and wonderfully made by the Lord. No matter what you look like.

And yes, there is a reason that when we eat whole foods that God put on the earth and we move our bodies regularly, we often do feel and look our best. But that feeling and looking our best can't be where we find our self-worth.

As we go through this chapter together, I want us to focus on diligently stewarding the temples God gave us so we can have energy to serve Him, live with purpose, and love people well. And yes, by taking these measures, you might feel more confident in the way you look, and that's okay too. But what's important is that you know that no matter how much you weigh, the Lord still sees you as His beautiful, precious daughter. And that's where your identity comes from.

What It Means for Your Body to Be a Temple

First Corinthians 6:19–20 says, "Do you not know that your bodies are temples of the Holy Spirit, who is in you, whom you have received from God? You are not your own; you were bought at a price. Therefore honor God with your bodies."

To understand the significance of equating your body with a temple, it's important to know the significance of the temple in the Old Testament.

The temple was the sacred place for the Israelites to meet with God. It was a physical holy place where the presence of God rested. During their travels in the wilderness, the Israelites carried a special tent called the tabernacle, which served as a portable temple.

When people wanted to be close to God, they went to the tabernacle, where His glory cloud rested. Though the Israelites could bring sacrifices to the tabernacle, only the priests could enter the tabernacle itself.

Later, when Jesus came to earth, He was the Messiah—the Son of God. God's presence dwelled in Him, and He became the fulfillment of the temple.

After Jesus beat death through His resurrection, that same Spirit became available to us. So, what was once something only the high priest could experience, now anyone can experience through a relationship with Jesus Christ. Because of Christ's sacrifice on the cross, the temple now is you, where God's Holy Spirit dwells the moment you choose to believe in Jesus and declare Him as Lord.

So, with this knowledge, it's important we treat our bodies well—as temples where the Holy Spirit dwells. That means we must pay attention to what we eat, practice self-control, and eat whole foods from God's green earth despite any temptation to stuff ourselves with junk food. We also must be active daily to keep our bodies healthy and moving well.

God knew what He was doing when He created us. It's

time we learned how to take care of our bodies in a way He designed for us to *thrive*.

How to Start Healthy Eating

When I knew it was time to start eating better, I prayed that God would help me make a commitment to choose to eat healthy food and that I would learn to enjoy the taste of whole foods. But after my experience with the cucumber and tomato salad, I felt a bit hopeless in trying to turn this area of my life around. You, too, may be struggling to actually enjoy healthy food, which tempts you to DoorDash Chick-fil-A or reach for a bag of chips instead.

One of the first successes on this journey came when I began to find new recipes with food that I looked forward to eating. Before long, I realized that I felt better and had more energy when prioritizing healthy eating. And bonus—I felt more confident in my own skin than I did before.

If you're ready to begin your own healthy eating journey, here are a few tips that could help.

1. Have Fun Making New Recipes

In my desperation for tasty food, I went on Pinterest and researched healthy recipes that I could cook and that looked appetizing. I followed recommendations from my favorite YouTubers and other content creators for quick, easy recipes that taste amazing and are also healthy.

With these recipes as a base, I began to just experiment in the kitchen.

Seeing which recipes I liked versus the ones that were a total flop became a fun little hobby. (Trust me, there were plenty of flops in this season of experimentation.)

I began making nutritious protein smoothies with fruit, nut butters, and yogurt. I created three-ingredient banana pancakes with just oats, bananas, and eggs. I got an air fryer and began to cook different meats and veggies. I made different sauces and used various spices so food would taste less bland. I sweetened breakfasts with pure maple syrup or honey instead of sugar.

And after a while, I started to enjoy the healthy foods much more than the junk food I was eating before.

Sometimes the most intimidating things for us are the things that are unfamiliar. For the longest time, I was so afraid of eating healthy and cooking because I didn't know much about them.

God bless my parents, but I grew up eating a lot of canned and packaged foods, which I think is quite common for people my age. Healthy eating has only recently become a huge focus in culture. For example, I never learned to like veggies when I was younger, because the ones I grew up eating would often go from frozen to cooked in only a minute, so they tended to taste very bland. Vegetables were boring. It was an association I had to overcome in my quest to eat better.

If that's your story, too, you must also break your preconceived notions. We must stop believing the lie that all healthy food tastes bad. God created food from the earth for us to enjoy and to nourish our bodies with what they need. The lie that "healthy food isn't for me" will prevent us from taking care of our bodies in the way God intended us to. If you truly want to start your health journey and step away from the junk food, make a commitment today to practice making new recipes. Start a Pinterest board, if you have to. And have fun with it.

If you need more suggestions on healthy recipes from God's green earth, you can always check out my Instagram (@ashleyhetherington). I also have a downloadable PDF cookbook, *Holy and Whole,* with more than sixty recipes that are yummy, healthy, and easy to make. You can access it here: thehoneyscoop.com/cookbook.

2. Don't Diss a Meal Plan

To achieve anything in life, a plan is pretty much essential.

When I started trying to eat better, I would go to the grocery store and buy all kinds of fruits and veggies—only to have them rot in the fridge because I never made a plan on how I would use them. Then I discovered meal planning, and it made all the difference.

Meal planning is a way for you to clearly decide what you'll be eating throughout the week (or other time period of your choice), making it easier to choose healthy food every day. It also helps you save money on groceries, because you won't be getting things you don't need that might otherwise go bad and have to be tossed out.

My meal planning process begins on the weekend. I'll go on Pinterest or watch my favorite YouTubers to get recipe inspiration. I'll typically write out two or three breakfasts and lunches and four dinners to cook throughout the week. I even plan my desserts.

I typically pull up the recipes on my phone, then copy the lists of ingredients and paste them into my grocery list in the Notes app. I make sure to delete any ingredient I know I already have in my fridge or pantry. This is all important prep work to do before heading to the grocery store so I don't buy more groceries than I need.

I sometimes cook dinner for my roommate. You might be cooking only for yourself, or maybe you have a whole family to feed. Obviously, based on the size of your household, you'll need to adjust the quantity of the groceries you buy for the meals you plan.

Meal planning helps with meal prep because I know exactly what I'm going to eat for the week, so I don't have to think about it each day. There is such a thing as decision fatigue—which happens when you feel overwhelmed by all the decisions you need to make. After a long day, it can be tempting to just order Chick-fil-A rather than to think about how you're going to include protein, fat, carbs, and greens from the leftovers in your fridge. If I have to think too much about something, it makes me not as likely to do it. Sticking to my plan helps me avoid overeating, keeps me on track with my health goals, and reduces the daily need to think about what I should eat.

In his book *Think Ahead,* Craig Groeschel talks about "the power of pre-decision," which is the practice of making a plan ahead of time to reduce the number of decisions you need to make.[1] When you pre-decide what meals you will make for the week, it will help you be more consistent with your decision to live a healthy lifestyle, as well as limit your chances of getting in your car and opting for fast food. For your healthy living journey, meal planning is a must.

3. Understand the Nutrients Your Body Needs

When I began my healthy eating plan, I read that I needed to build a "healthy eating plate."[2] Building a healthy, balanced meal is about filling your plate with the right macronutrients to give you energy (more on this later), balance your blood sugar, and give your body what it needs to thrive. Because I wasn't taught how to build a balanced plate in school or at home, I had to learn how to do this on my own. I want to share what I learned so you don't have to go through all the research I did. I hope I can serve you as a mentor holding your hand—like the one I wish I'd had when I was younger.

If you don't have a clue where to begin in building your plate, know that you are not alone in this! My roommate, Ally, didn't know how to properly fuel her body either until her late twenties. She would often not eat until dinnertime, and then once that time rolled around, she would load up on heavy carbs because she was ravenous from not taking the time to make herself a meal all day. She felt that would keep her full until the next evening.

But after I walked Ally through the process of building a balanced plate and eating three meals a day, she lost fifteen pounds. She lost weight by *eating more*. This is likely because skipping meals can slow down your metabolism, which can lead to weight gain or make it harder to lose weight. When you aren't giving your body enough fuel, it doesn't know when it's going to get food next, so it holds on to those calories to conserve energy. Eating more balanced meals throughout the day can boost metabolism and improve energy levels, which contributes to weight loss. When you support your body with enough calories and nutrients to give it energy and make it feel safe, it can thrive and look its best too.[3]

When building a balanced plate, I typically consider putting these three macronutrients on it: protein, healthy fat, and carbs. Macronutrients, or macros, are "nutrients that your body needs in large amounts to function optimally." They provide your body with what it needs to maintain its structure and functions. If you incorporate a good balance of carbs, fat, and protein into your daily diet, it will give you energy, regulate blood sugar, and even build and repair tissues. This all supports your body so you can be in a place for optimal health.[4]

Let's look at these macronutrients in more detail. What you'll see below is that, from the earth, God created all these foods that serve our bodies' needs and help our bodies run the way He intended for them to run.

PROTEIN

Protein is especially important for building and repairing muscle. It supports our hair, bones, and other tissue. It helps repair our cells and even aids in making new ones. Protein strengthens our immunity, allowing us to fight off colds and other viruses. Additionally, it has a high thermogenic effect, meaning it takes more energy for our bodies to break protein down (compared with other macros), which burns more calories. More protein helps balance blood pH, curbs appetite, and lowers blood pressure.[5]

Here are some examples of protein to include in your diet:

- eggs
- wild-caught fish
- grass-fed beef
- Greek yogurt
- chicken
- protein powder
- turkey
- nuts
- tuna
- beans and lentils
- tofu
- chickpeas
- shrimp

When it comes to portion sizes, it's recommended to eat 0.36 grams of protein per pound of your body weight each day. I suggest keeping that number in the back of your head to help you build your meals with the amount of protein your body needs. If you don't hit your protein goal for the day, it's not the end of the world. But when you can, aim to get a good amount of protein in each meal.

FAT

Fat isn't something for you to be afraid of in your diet. I used to always opt for fat-free foods until I realized that God created healthy fat to ensure our bodies work properly.

Healthy fat is needed for hormone regulation and nutrient absorption. It provides energy and aids in proper cell function.[6]

Here are some examples of fat to include in your diet:

- avocado
- nuts
- seeds
- oils, including coconut oil
- dark chocolate (85 percent or more cacao)
- nut butters

CARBOHYDRATES

Similar to fats, carbohydrates often get a bad rap. But carbs are very important in our daily diet. They serve as the body's primary source of energy, especially complex carbohydrates, which provide sustained energy release. You shouldn't be afraid of carbs, because complex carbs like fruits, veggies, and whole grains are packed with fiber, essential nutrients, and antioxidants. They keep you satiated (which means you feel full), suppressing the urge to run back for seconds. About 45 to 65 percent of our daily calories should come from carbs.[7]

Here are some examples of carbohydrates to include in your diet:

- sweet potatoes
- white potatoes
- fruits
- oats

- brown rice
- quinoa
- beans and lentils
- sourdough bread
- whole grain cereal
- whole wheat pasta

FIBER

When you think of fiber, think of your fruits and veggies. Fiber is a type of carb that your body can't break down well. I love fiber because it improves gut health, helps remove waste from the body, regulates blood sugar, lowers cholesterol, supports strong immunity, helps control your appetite and promote weight loss, helps prevent diabetes and other diseases, and may even benefit your mood. It also can reduce your risk of cancer, especially colon cancer.[8]

Here are some examples of fiber to include in your diet:

- vegetables: brussels sprouts, broccoli, carrots, cauliflower, green beans, sweet potatoes, kale, bell peppers, spinach, tomatoes, zucchini, lettuce, mushrooms, asparagus
- nuts and seeds: almonds, chia seeds, sunflower seeds, Brazil nuts
- fruits: strawberries, bananas, apples, avocado, raspberries, mango, blueberries
- grains: oats, quinoa, whole wheat pasta, brown rice
- beans and lentils
- chickpeas

GREENS

This is a great bonus to building a balanced plate. Greens might not be something you always look forward to or something you want to include in every meal, but they have incredible health benefits that we can't ignore. Greens are an amazing source of vitamins and minerals. When you have an adequate quantity of greens, your body functions optimally. Greens boost immunity, promote heart health, improve bone health, support eye health, reduce cancer risk, improve digestion, provide energy, and support healthy skin.[9]

Here are some examples of greens to include in your diet:

- kale
- spinach
- zucchini
- broccoli
- lettuce
- cucumber

4. Build a Balanced Plate

When it comes to how much a person should eat, everyone is unique. This is why it's beneficial to work with a registered dietician or a personal trainer, based on the goals you have, to make sure you're properly nourishing your body.

However, there are some basic principles that apply to anyone. For starters, you can look at your plate and consider . . .

- What is my protein source?
- What is my healthy fat?
- What is my healthy carb/fiber?
- What is my green of choice?

Nutritionist Kelly LeVeque has a principle called the Fab Four. She advocates for building your plate around a good protein, healthy fat, fiber (carbs), and greens. Incorporating these four foods into your daily meals will boost your energy, keep you satisfied, and help you shed extra pounds. As she explains, eating according to this principle helps us "keep energy consistent throughout the day, avoiding insulin spikes that tell our bodies to stop burning fat and start storing it."[10]

When I used to overeat during meals, I wasn't creating a balanced plate. Once I started including what my body truly needs—good protein, healthy fat, healthy carbs, and vegetables (greens)—I felt satisfied after eating and didn't feel hungry again a half hour later. Many of us are hungry and tired all the time because we aren't adequately fueling ourselves with the nutrients we need in each meal.

When you're making your meal plan for the week, you can keep this formula in mind and make sure you're hitting these four nutrient groups in each of your meals. If you build a balanced plate for each meal of the day, you will feel full for hours on end and energized until your next meal.

How to Resist Cravings

One of the biggest questions I get is how to resist cravings for junk food and sugar. And I understand, as this was a huge struggle for me too. Even just the other day at the grocery store, I gave in to my weakness: a big slice of carrot cake. I ended up eating the whole slice in one sitting, and my tummy didn't feel good afterward. I felt a huge crash of energy and was completely stuffed.

What I could have done instead is have a few bites of the carrot cake, until I felt full. And then put the rest away for when I wanted to have dessert next.

There's a beautiful fruit of the Spirit in Galatians 5:23 called self-control. And as we learn to eat healthy, we are learning to have self-control with food as well.

Here are just a couple of things that have helped me build self-control around food.

1. Pre-Decide Your Meals

We've already discussed the importance of meal planning, but just to recap, when you plan meals for the week and know what you'll cook and eat for each one, it's easier to resist the urge to get fast food.

2. Remember "Out of Sight, Out of Mind"

My parents loved to buy cookies when I was growing up. They would put them out on the kitchen island every day, making them hard to resist because they were always in plain view. The idea of "out of sight, out of mind" in healthy eating suggests that by keeping cookies, cakes, and other unhealthy foods hidden, you're less likely to eat them since they're not constantly on your mind.

Instead, keep healthy foods visible or easily accessible, like in the front of your fridge. The foods you see the most are most likely going to be the ones you eat the most. So put away those cookies that are on the counter and replace them with apples or bananas instead.

3. Follow the 80/20 Rule

When I began my health journey, I promised myself that I wasn't going to eat any ice cream, cake, or cookies. But when these types of food were in front of me after I'd deprived myself for so long, I had a stronger temptation to grab what wasn't good for me—and to eat way too much of it—not knowing the next time it would be available.

Now I'm an advocate of the 80/20 rule. (I don't love calling it a rule—it's more like a method for balanced healthy eating.) This is where 80 percent of the time you eat healthy foods that will fuel your body best and help you feel your best, such as by including the big three on your plate.

But then 20 percent of the time, you're able to enjoy other foods in moderation so you won't feel deprived or driven to overeating. This approach makes this new lifestyle realistic, which helps you commit to long-term healthy eating rather than adopting an all-or-nothing mindset. This flexibility to enjoy foods freely allows you to indulge in a cookie or carrot cake, knowing that you've already met your nutritional needs for most of the week.

The 80/20 rule is a plan for healthy eating that doesn't feel like a restrictive diet—where you can't ever enjoy the rigatoni or the carrot cake.

When I implement this method, I focus on meal planning Monday through Friday. But then I leave room on the weekend to go to dinner with my friends or to enjoy some ice cream at my favorite local shop.

4. Learn to Eat Intuitively

"Eating intuitively is about choosing foods that satisfy both your health needs and your taste buds."[11] It's not just about how something's going to taste but also about how it's going to make you feel.

The other day I was at a post-church lunch. Two things caught my eye: the spicy rigatoni and the ahi tuna salad. Everyone around the table was talking about how they were craving some pasta. And yes, I absolutely love spicy rigatoni. But then I thought about how eating heavy pasta in the middle of the day would make me *feel*. I didn't want to feel lethargic for the rest of the day. Instead, I wanted to have energy for a productive Sunday so I could get my groceries and plan my week.

I ended up getting the ahi tuna salad, and it was absolutely delicious. The mix of greens, protein, avocado, and mango was so refreshing to my taste buds and gave me a ton of energy. I was the only one eating a salad—while my friends around me all ate their pasta.

After we finished eating, my friends complained about feeling stuffed and not so good. Meanwhile, I felt like a million bucks.

I'm not dissing on eating pasta. In moderation, I think you can truly enjoy any food at any time, and I don't think you should restrict yourself.

But a mindset shift that helped me make healthier choices was considering, How will this food make me *feel*?

Another part of intuitive eating is listening to your body's natural cues of hunger and fullness. So, in this case, eat the pasta when you feel like eating pasta. Eat slowly and pay attention to when you're getting full. When you reach the point of fullness, you can put the fork down and acknowledge you're full. If you want to save the pasta for later, you can do that too. Same thing goes for eating cake. Pay attention to what your body is telling you; eat when you're hungry; stop when you're full. Your body will tell you what it needs.

This helped me cut down on mindless snacking when I wasn't actually hungry. It helped me take a few bites of a cookie instead of having two cookies, because I knew I needed more fuel for the day rather than a crash. And instead of going into my workout without any food at all, I'll fuel my body with yogurt and fruit to have more energy to move. I started seeing food as a way to take care of my body and give it the fuel it needs.

5. Opt for Healthier Desserts

Of course, there is room in your life for desserts that add no nutritional value to your meals. But something I've adopted more regularly is making desserts with healthier ingredients.

I find when I eat desserts made with mostly whole-food ingredients, they help me feel satisfied after eating them—versus having a need to finish the whole bag of M&M's with a lot of added sugar.

Here are some simple desserts that are my go-to on typical nights:

- Dark chocolate (a great source of healthy fat!)
- Ninja CREAMi: Blend peanut butter protein powder with milk. Let freeze for twelve to twenty-four hours. Spin in your Ninja CREAMi ice-cream maker, then add toppings like dark chocolate and peanut butter to make it taste like chocolate peanut butter cup ice cream.
- Dates with almond butter and dark chocolate, topped with a dash of cinnamon
- Bone broth hot chocolate: Mix together 1 cup milk, 1 cup bone broth, 1 tbsp cacao powder, 1 tbsp maple syrup, ½ scoop collagen, and a pinch of salt, then microwave or heat on the stovetop.
- Yogurt parfait: Top Greek yogurt with granola, fresh berries, and melted dark chocolate. Pop it in the freezer for fifteen minutes until the chocolate hardens.

Overcoming Temptations

I'd be lying if I said I'm never tempted to reach for a box of cookies when I'm feeling sad or anxious or for a bag of chips when I'm stressed out or when it's that time of the month.

I'll never suggest you can't enjoy these foods ever either. But there's a difference between enjoying a food and going to that food for the comfort that God wants to give.

When I'm tempted to eat junk food to numb feelings, here are some of the things that always help.

1. Speak Scripture over Your Identity

Scripture is a mighty weapon we can use under temptation. Ephesians 6:17 instructs, "Put on salvation as your helmet, and take the sword of the Spirit, which is the word of God" (NLT). This scripture emphasizes that our weapons are spiritual rather than physical. Since we face demonic spiritual forces, it stands to reason that our defense would be of the Spirit. So, when we face temptations like gluttony, we need to use the Word of God as our weapon.

For me, using the Word of God as a sword means declaring biblical truths out loud over my identity. Here are a few you can have on hand the next time you are tempted:

- God has not given me a spirit of fear, but of power, love, and self-discipline (2 Timothy 1:7, NLT).
- My body is a temple of the Holy Spirit. I was bought with a price. Therefore, I will honor God with my body (1 Corinthians 6:19–20).
- God is faithful to me. He will not allow this temptation to be more than I can stand. He will show me a way out so that I can endure (1 Corinthians 10:13, NLT).

The best way to wield the sword of the Spirit—the Word of God—as your weapon is to take scriptures that are applicable to your situation and make them into declarations.

2. Ask God for Help with That Temptation

When you are done using the sword of the Spirit, which is the Word of God, it's time to pray. Ephesians 6:18 supports this: "Pray in the Spirit at all times and on every occasion. Stay alert and be persistent in your prayers for all believers everywhere" (NLT).

Prayer is your superpower. And you don't need to be fancy about prayer. When I'm tempted to fall into gluttony or grab a cookie instead of a salad, I will simply ask God, "What do You want me to eat right now, Lord?"

When I listen for His answer, sometimes the Spirit will bring to my mind the emotion I'm feeling and will remind me to bring it to Him instead of the pantry. Other times the Spirit will remind me that I haven't had enough water today and that's really what my body is craving.

When I invite God into my decisions with food, He genuinely helps me decide what to eat—and when to go to Him instead of turning to food.

Ask God to show you the way out of the temptation, and He will be faithful to do just that.

3. Think About Your Future Self

When I'm tempted to eat foods that I know aren't the best for me, I find it helpful to think how my future self will be affected. I imagine what would happen if, for the next six months, I instead diligently took care of myself and chose to eat healthy foods from the earth over junk food 80 percent of the time. I think about how much better I will feel and how much more energy I will have. Picturing a future version of myself gives me the motivation to resist short-term gratification for long-term gain.

To treat my body as a temple, not only do I need to feed it properly, but I must also exercise it well. Let's talk about that next.

The Importance of Movement

Working out can be intimidating. Especially if you are just starting out and you haven't really gotten into the habit of moving your body.

Growing up, I was involved in sports, but when I got to college, I was unsure about what to do at the gym. Sometimes I would walk on the treadmill, then follow up with an ab exercise. Other times I would run until I got tired. Or I would try to work on the machines at the gym, not having a clue what I was doing. I didn't enjoy it and I wasn't consistent.

In order for me to be committed to exercise, God had to take me on a journey of learning how to steward my body through daily movement that I actually enjoyed, instead of working out being something I didn't really look forward to.

I believe God created exercise because of the many benefits it has on our physical and mental health. If He never wanted us to exercise, then why would it be so beneficial to our bodies? Exercise fights health conditions, improves mood, boosts energy, promotes better sleep, and controls weight.[12] There is a reason God describes the Proverbs 31 woman as a woman of strength. I love the AMPC version of Proverbs 31:17–18: "She girds herself with strength [spiritual, mental, and physical fitness for her God-given task] and makes her arms strong *and* firm." In Scripture we see that a woman of God is far from weak.

So, if you want to start moving your body regularly and you are lacking motivation, I hope these tips will help you.

1. Find Workouts You Enjoy

My roommate, Ally, is stepping into her workout era. We thought a good way for her to get started was to just walk on the treadmill while listening to worship music. When she came home from going to the gym after her walking sessions, she was in the worst mood. One day she looked at me and said, "I hate the gym."

I pressed in and asked why she hated it—only to find out that what she really hated was walking on a treadmill for forty-five minutes. Although walking regularly is a great way to ease into your fitness journey, Ally had no interest in staring into nothingness and walking for almost an hour. In order for her to enjoy going to the gym, we needed to find workouts she liked.

Not everyone enjoys the same type of workout. I have a friend who loves doing CrossFit at dawn, another who loves a regular six-mile run, and another who could do Pilates every single day and be happy. Each of these friends has found a workout that they look forward to and that feels best for their body.

So, in order to start working out, experiment with different types of workouts. Here are some you could try:

- Pilates
- running
- walking
- strength training
- boxing
- HIIT
- CrossFit

2. Commit to a Schedule

Remember when we talked about having a Bible reading plan? And a meal plan? Well, the same goes for having a workout plan.

If you fail to plan, you plan to fail.

For us to succeed at anything in life, it's important we have a plan of action to help us be consistent.

My workout schedule differs depending on the week, but typically it looks like three or four strength training days because I find my body responds well to lifting weights and I want to be strong and live a long life. Along with my strength training days, I aim for one or two Pilates days with light cardio sessions. And then each day I walk ten thousand to twelve thousand steps. I fit in two rest days a week.

This is what I find works best for me, helping me feel strong and energized but also helping me not overdo it and giving my body the rest it needs. But what works for me might not work for you. The key is finding what works for you and what workouts you enjoy.

When I tried CrossFit, I hated it, despite the fact that one of my best friends is a die-hard CrossFit fan. But when I do Pilates and lifting, I usually look forward to my workouts because they leave me feeling good and energized.

3. Pair Your Workouts with Something You Enjoy

Remember when we discussed James Clear's suggestion of temptation bundling, which is basically pairing a habit with something you already love? This philosophy can also be applied to workouts.

One thing I love is watching YouTube. I found that during my lifting sessions and treadmill walking, I can throw on a YouTube vlog and enjoy it as I work up a good sweat. I also love listening to worship music in the middle of a workout. You can even listen to the Bible app on your phone as you work out or go on a solid prayer walk, where you use that time to talk to God. You can grow in your faith as you move your body.

4. Stick with It

Too often we give up on something before we see the results. But committing to being faithful in the different areas of your life until you're able to see fruit is what the sowing season is all about.

When you come up with your workout plan, decide to stick with it. If you miss one day, decide that you won't miss two.

If you don't see results in the way you feel and if you hate every time you go to the gym, know that, with some things, you will enjoy them the more you do them. And the more you do those things, the easier they become.

Choose to stick with your workout routine and keep going. Slowly but surely, you will feel stronger and better as you choose to be consistent.

5. Have Accountability

Like with growing in your faith, having accountability with your workout goals can also help you be consistent with moving your body every day.

The husband of one of my church friends is involved in something called F3. It stands for "fitness, fellowship, faith." As my friend described it to me, it's like a secret club for men who meet outside in different cities at the crack of dawn to work out together. When men come to their first meeting, they are given a nickname, so rarely do they even know one another's names. But what's beautiful is these men get together in the early-morning hours to hold one another accountable, push one another closer to Christ, and help one another become the men that God created them to be.

When someone else is counting on you to show up, you won't want to let them down. When you schedule workout classes with your friend from church or you choose to go on a walk with a new friend from Bible study, not only are you moving your body, but you are also better stewarding your relationships. Going on walks and doing workouts with friends is such a great way to bond and to keep yourself committed to working out.

6. Choose Your Priorities

If you want to make stewarding your health a priority in this season, you must learn to say no to things that aren't as important to you.

My personal trainer tells me that if everything is a priority, nothing is a priority. (That might remind you of the principle from the last chapter: If you're focused on everything, you're focused on nothing.) There was a time when I got to one of our sessions and I was so overwhelmed by trying to juggle all the things I thought I needed to do. I was filled with so much stress and anxiety that I was on the verge of a panic attack.

She asked me then to write down my top priorities but to list only three. This was quite a bummer for me because at the time I wanted to have seven to ten priorities. Having only three felt very limiting.

But the truth is, we're all limited. We can't have ten priorities and do them all well.

The key is choosing few priorities but doing those with excellence and intentionality.

Get Your Sleep

If you recall my sleeping habits back in chapter 3, you won't be surprised that I used to stay up way too late only to feel frustrated when I was tired for my quiet time the next day. Somehow I could still function on little to no sleep. And because I could get through the day (not thrive—simply survive) on little sleep, I felt like it would be okay to keep this habit in my life. But just because you can do something doesn't mean you should.

I didn't fully appreciate the importance of sleep and didn't realize that getting only five or six hours a night was insufficient for the life God intended for me. It took me a long time to break this bad habit. Initially, I wrote down that one of my goals was to get more sleep, but I never took action to achieve it. I kept wondering why I couldn't be disciplined in waking up early, but my bad habits actually started the night before. To feel rested in the morning, I had to first focus on how I spent my evenings. It didn't matter how early I woke up or how well I executed my morning routine if I wasn't getting enough sleep and my nights were disorganized.

After repeatedly waking up exhausted, I realized deep down that I needed to make a change that would make my future self proud. I had to learn the true importance of sleep and how our bodies need it to function properly. It hasn't been easy to reach the point where I prioritize my nights, but I've learned so much over the years that has helped me create an evening routine that I can consistently follow and enjoy. This routine helps me stay faithful to the life God has called me to.

Why Sleep Is Good for You

There are countless benefits to getting good sleep. If you're like me, you might need someone to physically shake you and tell you why you can't keep living on little sleep.

Quality sleep boosts productivity, reduces the risk of depression and anxiety, lowers the risk of weight gain and obesity, and strengthens immunity.[13] And if you want to be a fit girly, getting enough sleep improves your ability to see results in the gym.

If the benefits aren't enough to convince you, let me tell you more about what happens when you don't get adequate sleep:

- **Forgetfulness:** Sleep helps us store information. When we don't sleep enough, we are more likely to forget things we would remember if we had slept for seven or eight hours.[14]
- **Skin issues:** Lack of sleep can cause fine lines and wrinkles or an uneven skin tone.[15]
- **Heart problems:** If you don't get enough sleep, it can cause increased risk of high blood pressure, strokes, and heart attacks.[16]
- **Diabetes risk:** Not sleeping enough can make your body less sensitive to insulin, which is a hormone that lowers your blood sugar levels.[17]
- **Hormonal imbalances:** The sleep cycle is directly linked to the body's natural hormone production. When you don't sleep enough, this can lead to fluctuations in hormones like cortisol, melatonin, leptin, and ghrelin. This negatively affects appetite, stress response, and metabolism.[18]
- **Irritability and mood swings:** You're more likely to wake up in a bad mood if you don't sleep well.[19]

Just looking at the cold, hard facts makes it clear that God created our bodies to run best off good sleep. I hope this is enough to convince you to get adequate rest—unlike me, who had to experience the consequences of this bad habit personally to really make a change.

God wants us to get good sleep. Psalm 127:2 says, "It is useless for you to work so hard from early morning until late at night, anxiously working for food to eat; for God gives rest to his loved ones" (NLT). He created us to need rest. And if we don't rest, unfortunately we will get to a place where our bodies will just shut down and we will be forced into rest.

Tips for Getting Adequate Sleep

If you need help in making changes with your sleep habits, let me give you the advice I wish I'd had ten years ago.

1. Give Yourself an End Time for Work

I work for myself, so this means I can basically work all the time because I don't have a boss to stop me. As I already said, some nights I would stay up editing videos until 2:00 A.M., which wasn't ideal for getting the sleep my body needed, especially if I also planned to wake up early. Even working until 8:00 P.M. was just not healthy and sustainable.

Because I never set a time when I would "clock out" for the day, I would just end up overworking and burning myself out. I would also go to bed at a different time every night, which wasn't helping me get into a good, healthy rhythm.

Giving myself a set time when I'm done with work has helped me be diligent in making sure I get all my work done during the day and don't procrastinate. Research backs this up. It shows that the more hours we work, the less productive we become.[20]

If you end the workday at a scheduled time, you will work more efficiently throughout the day. For me, I found that my sweet spot for ending work is around 4:30 or 5:00 P.M. Afterward, I immediately go on a prayer walk and respond to texts before I start cooking dinner. I'm proud to say my routine has changed a lot from those nights staying up editing videos until spooky hours.

2. Plan for the Next Day

Just before "clocking out" for the day, I always make sure to plan for the next day by opening my planner and writing out the top three things I will need to get done tomorrow. This way, when I start work the next day, I already know what to focus on. Usually, nothing is so urgent that it must be done today. Tasks can typically wait until the next day without any negative consequences.

3. Avoid Eating Late at Night

When I would work until eight, I wouldn't be able to eat dinner until eight-thirty or nine. But then I found out how unhealthy it is to go to bed with a full stomach, and realized I needed to change that habit.

When you're eating late, your body is focusing on digesting food rather than resting. This can cause you to wake up tired.

It's really important we allow our bodies to digest the food we eat before we go to sleep. You should finish your last meal two to three hours before going to bed.

I usually start cooking around five, after my afternoon walk, and I eat around six every night. This gives me plenty of time to digest dinner before bed.

4. Have a Nightly Routine You Look Forward To

If you want to master your sleep, you must also have a nightly routine you can be consistent with.

My nighttime routine consists of making dinner, taking a warm shower, doing skincare, drinking tea, and eating dark chocolate. Then I will typically take magnesium, cozy up in bed with a book, and go to sleep around ten.

Your night routine doesn't have to look like mine, but make sure you include relaxing activities that are going to help you go to bed at a consistent time.

5. Avoid Caffeine

I used to be the type of girl who would usually have at least three cups of coffee a day and drink her last cup in the middle of the afternoon. I relied on coffee to boost my productivity, and this led to a struggle to fall asleep at night.

Studies show that caffeine can disrupt sleep, even if you consume it several hours before you go to bed.[21]

Caffeine acts as a stimulant, blocking receptors in your

brain that promote sleepiness.[22] "You may experience the peak effects of caffeine 30–60 minutes after consuming it. However, caffeine can stay in your body for many hours after, which may affect your sleep."[23]

When I found out all of this, I knew I needed to reevaluate my caffeine habits.

Now I typically drink my last caffeinated beverage by noon so that enough of it is out of my system by the time my head is hitting the pillow. If I get a drink in the afternoon at a coffee shop or I make one at home, it's either decaf coffee or herbal tea.

In Los Angeles, matcha is all the rage, and as I mentioned earlier, I've switched my drink of preference from coffee to matcha to lower cortisol spikes. I limit it to one cup a day since it contains caffeine. The caffeine in a cup of matcha is about half what is in a cup of coffee.

I still have my dark chocolate at night, which contains a little bit of caffeine. But I aim to eat it a few hours before bedtime so that it doesn't affect me at night.

At night, I like to drink peppermint tea, ginger tea with lemon, or chamomile lavender tea. All are caffeine-free and each provides different health benefits.

In fact, drinking chamomile lavender tea before bed can help with sleep quality and relaxation. Both chamomile and lavender can reduce insomnia, anxiety, and stress.[24]

6. Take Magnesium Before Bed

I make sure to take magnesium thirty minutes to an hour before going to bed. When I discovered magnesium, I found that I got sleepier more quickly and I felt so much more rested in the morning. I learned that it has so many benefits, like regulating melatonin production, reducing the time it takes to fall asleep, and naturally improving your overall sleep quality.[25]

You can also follow the trend of a "sleepy girl mocktail," which is where you mix one tablespoon of magnesium powder with a half cup of pure tart cherry juice and top it off with sparkling water or a prebiotic soda.

7. Get Off Your Phone

Before I go to bed, I put my phone to sleep as well. It's important to put your phone away before bed because its blue light can disrupt your circadian rhythm, making it harder to fall asleep and wake up refreshed. Blue light inhibits melatonin, the hormone that regulates your sleep/wake cycle, tricking your brain into thinking it's daytime.[26] Having your phone near you also can disrupt your REM sleep because of notifications you get through the night. The National Sleep Foundation suggests putting away all electronic devices, including your phone, at least an hour before bedtime.[27]

For the most part, nothing is ever really urgent. Any notification that you are getting at night can most likely wait until the next morning.

Putting your phone away may feel difficult, but your body is going to thank you later. And TikTok can wait until the next day.

8. Read a Book (or the Bible)

I love reading a book before bed. My favorite thing is lighting a candle on my bedside table and flipping through a great book. Doing so helps me relax, reduces stress, and improves my sleep quality. I always find after I read for around fifteen or twenty minutes, my mind gets tired and lets me know it's time to fall asleep.

I also love reading a psalm from the Bible. If you ever have trouble sleeping, declare Psalm 91 over yourself and cling to the truth that God is protecting you with His angels. Bedtime is also a good time for me to journal so I don't have any thoughts swirling in my mind from the day. Journaling allows me to fall asleep with a clear mind.

And if you struggle to get in your quiet time during the morning hours, you can spend time with God at night instead.

9. Pray

Many people suggest meditation before bed, but my favorite thing to do is *pray*.

After I put my phone away and just about the time my magnesium has kicked in, I lie in bed and pray. I'll get thoughts and visions from the Lord, and He will just speak to me in that place. I feel the Lord lulls me to sleep. Lying in bed and praying at night is comforting.

10. Go to Bed at the Same Time Every Night

It's so important that we set a consistent bedtime and wake-up time. When you do this, your circadian rhythm will become fully stabilized, which will make you more energized during the day and more relaxed at night. It trains your brain to go to sleep and wake up at the same time without you even having to try.

This is why I've been able to consistently wake up early. I'm naturally getting tired at the same time every night, and my body naturally wants to get out of bed in the morning.

There is hope for you if you aren't a morning person. I wasn't either at first, and I swore I never would be. But I realized that it's as simple as training my body to go to bed early every night by putting these steps into practice, then having a consistent morning routine to look forward to.

Don't Forget to Hydrate

If we are mentioning other health tips, like sleeping, exercising, and eating healthy food, it's also important we mention the importance of drinking water. Over the past few years, huge water bottles have become very trendy. As I write this, my big Stanley cup is resting on my desk, a constant companion wherever I go.

But that wasn't always the case. I used to struggle to drink enough water throughout the day, simply because I didn't think it tasted good. I would have preferred Dr Pepper instead.

Eventually I realized that staying hydrated helps my body function properly. Without sufficient water, my body isn't getting the nutrients it needs and can't perform well.

Drinking water regulates your body temperature, helps your joints, brings nutrients to your cells, flushes out toxins, improves sleep, helps you think more clearly, and can affect your energy levels and mood. It can also aid in digestion and weight loss by helping you metabolize food more effectively and suppressing appetite.[28]

Not drinking enough water can lead to multiple health issues. Insufficient hydration can cause headaches, dizziness, and fatigue. In the long term, it can cause high blood pressure, muscle weakness, and joint pain and impair your memory and your ability to concentrate.[29]

As a helpful guideline, you can take your body weight in pounds and divide it by two to get the number of ounces you should be drinking each day.[30]

To incorporate this habit, I started drinking a glass of water as soon as I wake up. I begin immediately because, after a night's rest, our bodies are typically quite dehydrated since they have been working without water. Then I drink a Stanley in the morning, which gets me through my workout. I drink another Stanley during the day. And then to top it all off, I make it a goal to have one more Stanley by the end of the night. But often I don't finish it, because I've been drinking water all day.

I often add things to my water—partly for flavoring but also for health benefits. Sometimes after workouts, I add BCAAs (branched-chain amino acids). They help with muscle growth and repair and reduce muscle soreness. Sometimes I add electrolytes if I've had a good workout at the gym, and other times I'll add a debloat pack. There are a lot of things we can add to our water to give it more flavor. And of course, you can always squeeze a lemon into your water to make it taste good naturally.

Another thing that encourages hydration is buying a water

bottle you like. You'll be much more likely to use it and carry it with you.

Love the Way You Look

Sometimes it can be difficult to look at yourself and actually like what you see. I know I've had so many occasions when I've struggled to see myself the way God created me. I've looked in the mirror and picked apart everything about myself. I've been my harshest critic.

And it doesn't help that we are bombarded daily with images of what we "should" look like. We go on social media and can be tempted to compare ourselves with every other woman on the internet. Honestly, when I find myself tempted to covet someone else's appearance, it's not usually driven by a desire for health. This can quickly become an idol, a fixation on controlling something beyond what God intended for me to manage. But God showed me that instead of wishing my body looked like someone else's, it was a beautiful thing for me to accept and love the body He gave me. He made each of our bodies differently.

Something that gave me a lot of freedom was learning about set point theory.

Set point weight refers to the weight your body naturally tends to maintain, determined by both your heredity and your environment. If you find yourself super hungry all the time, it might be your body's way of telling you it needs more food to be at your set point weight. If you overeat, your body will cue its satiety signals to let you know it's had too much food for your set point weight.[31]

In my past, when I've been restricting my eating to try to look like someone I saw on social media, I've often not been at my set point weight. This put my body into starvation mode, prompting me to eat more. But on the other hand, if I eat too much for my body, it tells me to stop eating and get moving.

Your body is made by God, and only He determines the size of it. You can try to change it by not eating enough and over-exercising, but your body won't function properly and will alert you, saying it needs more nutrients.

When it comes to being faithful with our health, we want to steward our body as a temple, not an idol. We want to sow seeds of taking care of the body God gave us. But we never want to worship it or become obsessed with what it looks like.

I love what David says in Psalms:

> You created my inmost being;
> you knit me together in my mother's womb.
> I praise you because I am fearfully and wonderfully made;
> your works are wonderful,
> I know that full well. (139:13–14)

God knit you together in your mother's womb. He looks at you—every part of you—and says you are fearfully and wonderfully made.

He created your genes and pre-determined which family you would come from. He chose your skin tone, your eye color, your tummy, your legs, your arms—even the parts of you that you want to change the most.

I found freedom after learning to embrace the way God made me instead of trying to fit a mold that was never meant for me. I prayed a simple prayer, again and again:

God, help me see myself the way You see me.

I consistently prayed this over myself, and it helped me see myself in a new light. It's crazy how a simple prayer can create such life transformation.

My Experience with the Mirror

I went through a health challenge where I gained about fifteen pounds in the span of a month. It got to a point where I couldn't fit into my old clothes, and seeing my reflection in the mirror made me so sad. I realized I needed to break a lot of bad habits to truly love myself and see myself the way God sees me.

One of the habits I picked up over the years was body checking, and honestly, it's not something I'm proud of. A major form of body checking is when you keep looking at yourself in the mirror. I used to do it all the time—checking out my stomach and legs whenever I passed by a mirror. But let's be real: Staring at myself didn't actually make me look any better or skinnier. It's kind of like if you continually check your bank account. Checking your bank account repeatedly throughout the day serves no purpose in helping it grow.

What helps it grow is focusing on the habits that are needed to better that area of your life.

So instead of checking my body in the mirror, I put my focus toward what would help my body be the best it can be: moving it daily, eating healthy foods, and getting good sleep. I knew if I was sowing seeds of faithfulness in my health, I would eventually reap a harvest by liking the way I look in the mirror and feeling confident.

I also didn't want to give in to a spirit of vanity, which was being fed every time I obsessed over what I looked like.

I realized that words have power and I couldn't keep nit-picking my body in the mirror. So, I started using them to boost how I see myself, rather than to tear myself down. On sticky notes I wrote out declarations based on Scripture, then put them all over my mirror, calling it a "truth mirror." Here are a few of the declarations I wrote out:

- God says I am fearfully and wonderfully made. (Psalm 139:14)
- God made healthy food for me to enjoy. (Psalm 24:1)
- God handcrafted me in His image. I will not argue with my Creator about how He created me. (Isaiah 45:9)

Whenever a negative thought comes up, let's hit refresh by praying these scriptures over ourselves. Seriously, it's going to change how we see ourselves. Even just saying "God, help me see myself the way You see me" can make a big difference.

If you create a truth mirror, please take a photo and tag

me on your stories (IG: @ashleyhetherington). I love seeing who is doing this with me!

How to Be Faithful with the Body God Gave You

When I was struggling the most with my body image, it got so bad that I would just look at myself in the mirror and start crying. I couldn't even bring myself to try on clothes at the mall. This all happened after a guy I really liked rejected me, and for some reason, it made me feel like I had to change my body because he didn't choose me.

I finally reached a point where I was done with looking at myself in the mirror and hating what I saw. So I wrote down my plan to change things and stuck it next to my mirror to see it every day:

The way to food freedom:
Feed yourself healthy foods and follow your workout plan.
Stop nitpicking your body in the mirror.
Surrender your body to the Lord
and fix your mind on Jesus.

As I work on being faithful with my health, I have peace knowing that it's my job to feed myself healthy foods and follow my workout plan, and it's my job to sleep well and hydrate. But it's God's job to determine the size of my body.

It's my job to stop nitpicking my body in the mirror, but it's God's job to help me see myself the way He sees me.

It's my job to take care of my body as a temple of the Holy Spirit—and with that posture, I can surrender my body to the Lord and fix my mind on Jesus. And trust that He will determine what it's supposed to look like.

So maybe you are in a rough spot with liking what you see in the mirror. Maybe you are struggling to fit into your jeans. Maybe you aren't getting enough sleep, and you know things need to change.

It's time for you to be faithful with the body God gave you.

You can practice eating healthy and cooking new healthy recipes for yourself that are quick, easy, and yummy to make.

You can get into a habit of going to the gym and moving your body every week, trying different movements.

You can get into a habit of getting at least seven to eight hours of sleep at night, developing a night routine you won't want to skip.

And you can work on hydrating your body by having fun trying new electrolyte packs and BCAAs.

God wants you to enjoy taking care of the body He gave you.

And it's time you did just that.

8

Bearing the Weight of Waiting

BEING FAITHFUL DESPITE DISAPPOINTMENT

The other night I cried myself to sleep. I was about to go to a bachelorette party for the sixth time. I was getting more and more baby shower invitations. I realized I had been living in California for roughly a year and I hadn't been asked out on a single date.

As I mentioned earlier, I've been single for the past six years. I don't want to sound like a broken record, but it's one of my biggest insecurities. Because I come from a family of divorce, my heart has been in a tug-of-war, trying to believe God has redemption for me in this area of love and relationships.

Each January, I believe God is going to orchestrate my love story *this year* and bring a husband into my life. But then as each December rolls around, I feel the weight of disappointment creep in, and it's heavy.

I find myself tempted to settle. To scroll on every dating

app under the sun. To ask my friends if they know any eligible bachelors. To take things into my own hands.

To be completely honest, just this past year, I thought I met the guy that God had for me. We were really good friends at first, and it seemed like he was pursuing me. He would flirt with me and ask me to hang out. I told myself, *This is surely it.*

But he wasn't ever asking me out. He never once took me on a date.

Each time I *thought* he was going to ask me on a date and didn't, I would just pray and believe that it needed to happen in God's timing.

Then I found out he was pursuing a different girl. At first, I couldn't believe it. When I heard he was dating someone else, my knees hit the ground and I cried my heart out. I didn't want to accept what I was hearing. I know that sounds dramatic, but I really didn't see it coming at all.

After months of waiting for this guy to ask me out and really believing that it was going to happen, I was completely devastated.

The days and weeks following were hard and dark. I questioned if God even had a good guy for me to marry. I questioned if I needed to do something myself to make this happen. I questioned if God had forgotten about my prayers for my future husband.

And as I attended all these weddings by myself, I kept believing that, by the next wedding, I would surely have someone. Each time it didn't happen left me feeling more hopeless.

I had to make a decision. Was I going to let this disappointment have the last word in my story, or would I let God have the last say? The choice was mine to make.

If Something Isn't Good, God Isn't Done

I firmly believe that if something isn't good, God isn't done.

Over the weeks after my heartbreak, I chose to not look inward anymore. Instead, I would look to God.

I remembered a line from the movie *The Shack:* "When all you see is your pain, you lose sight of Me."[1] This was me. I was so focused on my singleness and my heartbreak that I completely lost sight of the God who was in control of my love story.

I had to seek God and bring all my thoughts, my hurt, my fears, to the feet of Jesus. I begged God to give me clarity on what on earth just happened. I asked Him to guide me and to help me believe again that He will provide a breakthrough and lead me to my spouse. I begged God to give me fresh hope, because I sure did need it.

I was desperate. But in my desperation, I ran to God. And I asked Him to show up.

Hearing God's Voice in the Waiting

When you're waiting for a promise from God, it's often not all sunshine and roses. It can feel like you don't have any control at all.

But nothing is a surprise to God. Not even the disappointments you go through. Whether you're waiting for a husband, a baby, or a job, bring those things to the feet of Jesus. God wants to speak to you in the waiting. He wants to guide you and show you that He is the one who has a plan.

When I began to seek God in my heartbreak by this boy, God showed me why it hadn't worked out. He gave me dreams and visions of why we wouldn't be the right match. He gave Ally similar dreams and visions on my behalf. I also had friends speak over me that despite there being many counterfeit companions, God had the perfect match. And I would just need to wait on His timing and trust that He was going to do it.

I also realized that if God wanted me to be with someone, I would be. And there is a reason He wants my time to go to ministry and business. If I had a husband and kids, my time would be divided and I wouldn't have the capacity to chase after the purpose God has given me.

I had to turn from looking inward at my own thoughts to letting God be the one to speak. I needed to trust that He did have a plan for the waiting period after all.

If you're in a waiting season, ask God to give you insight and guidance. He tells us to trust Him with all our hearts and lean not on our own understanding (Proverbs 3:5–6). Instead of asking God "Why?" ask Him those two simple questions we mentioned in chapter 6:

1. God, what do You want me to know?
2. God, what do You want me to do?

God wants to speak to you in the waiting. And He wants to give you hope in your disappointment.

Comparison Is the Thief of Joy

When we find ourselves struggling to wait for the Lord and His perfect timing, it can be tempting to fall into the trap of comparing our lives with those around us.

We might see baby shower invitations and wonder when it will be our turn.

Seeing friends getting married might make us feel we're behind in life because we aren't in that same season.

Witnessing someone else advance in their career can leave us feeling overlooked in the job we show up for every day.

I'll be the first to admit that I've often felt tempted to compare myself with others. I wonder if I've somehow missed out on the plans God has for me, because I feel behind in life.

In moments when I find myself comparing my life with others', I must repent and turn to the truth found in God's Word. The notion that God has abandoned me or that He cares more about everyone else is a lie.

I have to align myself with the truth:

God has a beautiful plan for me, to give me a hope and a future (Jeremiah 29:11).

God is guiding my steps to align with His perfect will (Proverbs 16:9) as I trust and submit to His purpose for my life (3:5–6).

God hears the cries of my heart and will save me from my troubles (Psalm 34:17).

The enemy can't make me compare my life with others. But if I'm in a vulnerable spot, I must be aware of the temptation to fall into the sin of comparison. I have to guard against this temptation, avoid social media, and focus on what God is asking me to do.

What we must realize about comparison is that the grass isn't *always* greener.

I find myself comparing my life with the lives of many married people, wishing I was in their shoes. Yet those same married people might be looking at me, wishing they were in mine.

We are never quite content. Even when we get to the season we always dreamed of, we'll find yet *another* thing we are forced to wait on. The best thing we can do is focus on where God has placed us and make the most of where we are.

I love *The Message* translation of 1 Corinthians 7:17: "Don't be wishing you were someplace else or with someone else. Where you are right now is God's place for you. Live and obey and love and believe right there. God, not your marital status, defines your life."

When we focus on everyone else's lives, we lose sight of being faithful stewards of the time and other gifts God has entrusted to us. Comparison robs us of the ability to focus on what God has given us in the season we are in, and we instead fixate on what we don't have.

The devil knows that focusing on being faithful with what God has entrusted to you is often the key to unlocking the next phase of your life. So, if the enemy can divert your attention from what God has given you, he can limit your impact now and in the future. This is the lesson in the parable of the talents. The servant given one talent compared himself with the others who received more and figured that what he had didn't really matter. His one talent lay dormant in the ground, and his master wasn't pleased with that.

You might have what looks like one talent right now. Maybe what God has given you feels small and meaningless in comparison with what He's given others. But He has still given you something to work with. And it's up to you if you are going to let that gift go to waste or if you are going to invest it and see Him use it for good.

I could have spent the past six years of singleness focusing on my engaged friends and convinced myself I needed to get married too. But instead, in my worst moments of comparison, the Lord encouraged me to focus on what He has given me. The past six years He has given me time, energy, and other resources to pour into my online ministry, my business, and my writing. If I had waited until after I got married to start on these dreams, I wouldn't be writing this book to you today.

God blesses your obedience. Look at the gifts He has given you, even if they are small. He wants you to invest what He has put in your life so that it will produce an abundant return for your future.

It All Comes Down to Trust

Through all my long nights of crying, through all my feelings of lack and disappointment, through the heartbreak and grief of watching something I thought was going to happen fall apart in front of my face . . . I had to make a decision.

Would I cling to my own understanding, or would I trust God?

Trusting God is believing in His power, reliability, and love, even in the most difficult circumstances.

I realized years into my Christian walk that even though I said I was a Christian and loved Jesus, I still wanted to be the author of my life. I still wanted control. But to love Jesus and give our lives to Him means to surrender to Him and give Him the pen to write our stories.

Amid my disappointment, I had to decide to trust God to answer my prayers and deliver on my dreams, no matter how many times I laid them at His feet and told Him to take them away from me.

I had to trust that God's promises would come to pass and that I wouldn't have to make things happen on my own. I had to trust His perfect timing, not my own preference. I had to trust Him even when I had no idea what was next.

And in that trust, I had to seek His will in the season He put me in and focus on being obedient to Him.

I'm now at a place where I trust God completely to write my love story. I trust Him to lead me in my dreams that simply haven't gone away. I trust His ability to be the author of my life and not my ability to make things happen in my own strength.

Circle of Influence Versus Circle of Concern

When your heart is truly in a place of trusting God, you can put your attention on being faithful with where God has you.

Whatever you cultivate grows. When you are faithful to sow in different areas of your life, you will be guaranteed to see growth.

We are in the business of effort, and the Lord is in the business of results.

A difficult thing about waiting on God is we are often waiting on things that are completely out of our control. But the Lord has given us things that we can still control, like being obedient and faithful with the lives we are living today.

In his book *The 7 Habits of Highly Effective People,* Stephen Covey talks about two kinds of people: proactive people, who focus on "the things they can do something about," and reactive people, who focus on "circumstances over which they have no control." Covey suggests that seeing success and change in our lives is dependent on focusing on what we can influence.

The more you focus on what you can control, the more you will be able to be faithful in your life and the more of a harvest you will reap. But if you focus all your energy on your circle of concern—the things you can't control—then your circle of influence will shrink. Proactive people will see that their circle of influence will increase.[2]

Here are some of the things that are in your circle of influence (what's yours to control):

- working hard
- being consistent
- tending to your relationship with God
- persevering
- innovating

- having a positive attitude
- putting yourself out there
- being a good friend
- loving those around you well

In contrast, here are the types of things that are in your circle of concern (what's not yours to control):

- results
- success
- the competition
- other people's decisions
- world events
- how others react
- what others think of you
- the weather

When you are in a place where it feels like God isn't turning to the next page of your life, you must focus on what's in your circle of influence—what you can control and remain faithful to—while you wait for Him to lead you to what's next.

God Will Reward Your Trust

If you're feeling stuck today, know that God sees you. No matter how discouraged you feel, He has a plan for you.

When nothing makes sense, that is an opportunity for us to trust God more. Maturing in your faith is realizing that you can trust God, no matter what happens. You can trust that His promises will come to pass in your life and that you don't have to do it on your own.

He has a good plan for your life. And as that good plan unfolds, you can be faithful exactly where He has put you today.

Your everyday faithfulness won't go to waste. Whether you are making the decision to be faithful to show up to a new Bible study, when you don't have any Christian friends . . .

Whether you are making the decision to be faithful to wake up early and read your Bible, when it seems boring and you don't understand it all . . .

Whether you are making the decision to show up to the gym and get stronger, when you feel like you could barely lift a single weight . . .

God sees your daily acts of faithfulness.

And you must remember, no matter how far away the breakthrough seems—eventually, you will see it, if you keep going.

The devil will try to get you to stop, because he knows if he can get you to give up, he can keep you from the harvest that's about to come. So don't let the devil win. Don't let your setback have the last say. No matter how discouraging things may seem, no matter how much it feels like you are waking up to the same day, no matter how many disappointments you face.

You are not giving up.

You will remain faithful. You won't stop until you see God move. You won't stop watering the seed God gave you to plant until you see the beautiful harvest He has promised you.

You get to make the decision whether you will move forward into the promises of God, with your eyes fixed on Jesus, or whether you will quit before you see the breakthrough.

But you won't ever see results if you quit right now. So decide to stay faithful and keep going.

You will surely reap a harvest of blessing. And that harvest could come much sooner than you think.

Acknowledgments

I'd like to offer my biggest thanks to all my friends and family who made this book possible.

Mom, thank you for encouraging me to never give up my dream of writing. It's because of you that this book even exists today. Dad, thank you for your constant encouragement as I wrote this book. You are such a gift in my life, and I am truly blessed to be your daughter.

Rachel Jacobson, my agent, thank you for being such an incredible agent and for encouraging me to turn this message into a book. You are an amazing advocate, and it's been a gift to be on this journey with you.

Susan Tjaden, you make writing such a joy. Thank you for investing your time, energy, and love in this project with me. It's wonderful creating books with you!

Campbell Wharton, Johanna Inwood, Jessica Kastner, and the whole team at WaterBrook, I am in awe of your passion and drive to put meaningful books in the hands of readers around the world. You put God first in your work, and it's a blessing to partner with you on this writing journey.

Ally Yost, Julie and Chris Bennett, Holly and Scott Reed, Marla Steel, and my many other friends in my community in Los Angeles, thank you for being with me through this whole writing process. I love getting to run alongside you all.

Emily Billman, Kelsey High, Kat Mena, Alyssa Brooks, Lindsey Nelson, Elisa Iglesia, and Molly Mendelson, thank you for sticking by my side since college. You all have been there since day one, when I started my writing journey. I wouldn't be here without your support over the years and am so thankful for each one of you.

Jazzy Chandler, Dana Novales, Sam Al-dossary, Makena Spellman, and the rest of Team Honey, I am so grateful for each of you who work so hard to bring encouraging content to our community every day. Working is so enjoyable because I get to pursue this mission alongside you.

To our incredible online community connected through YouTube, TikTok, Instagram, Pinterest, and our newsletter, thank you for living life with me every day and being on this journey with me. Thank you for allowing me to pour into your life over the years to help you grow closer to Jesus. I am so grateful to have you in this community.

And last but certainly not least, thank You, God, for never giving up on me and always leading me. I pray this book brings glory to You.

Notes

CHAPTER 2: LETTING THE WORD OF GOD TRANSFORM YOU

1. James Clear, *Atomic Habits: An Easy & Proven Way to Build Good Habits & Break Bad Ones* (Avery, 2018), 99–112.
2. The Tree is a paid monthly subscription with Zoom calls, Bible plans, and other resources. For more information, go to thehoney scoop.com/tree.
3. "SOAP Bible Study Method," SOAP Studies, soapstudies.com/ soap-bible-study-method.
4. Clear, *Atomic Habits,* 72–74, 108–9.

CHAPTER 3: BUILDING SPIRITUAL RESILIENCE

1. Often attributed to Jim Rohn.
2. Craig Groeschel, *The Power to Change: Mastering the Habits That Matter Most* (Zondervan, 2023), 16.
3. Groeschel, *The Power to Change,* 17.

CHAPTER 4: NAVIGATING THE WILDERNESS OF LONELINESS

1. *American Gangster,* directed by Ridley Scott (Universal Pictures and Imagine Entertainment, 2007).
2. C. S. Lewis, *Mere Christianity* (HarperOne, 2001), 226–27.

CHAPTER 6: PLANTING FOR THE FUTURE

1. "Building and Sustaining Momentum: A Key of Your Business Success," *CIO Views,* cioviews.com/building-and-sustaining-momentum-a-key-of-your-business-success.
2. The Hebrew word for "wilderness" is *midbar* (מִדְבָּר), and it comes from the root word *dabar* (רַבָּד), which means "to speak." This etymological connection is often interpreted to suggest that the wilderness is a place where God communicates with people. Jennifer Gross, "Listening to the Lord in the Wilderness," Concordia Publishing House (blog), October 4, 2021, blog.cph.org/read/listening-to-the-lord-in-the-wilderness. See also *Theological Dictionary of the Old Testament,* edited by G. Johannes Botterweck and Helmer Ringgren, which explores the roots and meanings of Hebrew words in depth.
3. Jamie Winship, "Learning Your True Identity (with Jamie Winship)," interview by Eryn Eddy and Elisa Morgan, hosts, *God Hears Her,* podcast, season 7, episode 116, Our Daily Bread Ministries, January 30, 2023, youtube.com/watch?v=WUcjWEOExUw&t=1647s.
4. Winship, "Learning Your True Identity."
5. Strong's Exhaustive Concordance, s.v. "85. Abraham," Bible Hub, biblehub.com/hebrew/85.htm.
6. Topical Lexicon, s.v. "sarah," Bible Hub, biblehub.com/hebrew/8282.htm.
7. Often attributed to Darren Hardy, a speaker and author known for helping leaders and other high achievers make an impact.

8. Craig Groeschel, *The Power to Change: Mastering the Habits That Matter Most* (Zondervan, 2023), 90.
9. James Clear, *Atomic Habits: An Easy & Proven Way to Build Good Habits & Break Bad Ones* (Avery, 2018), 27.
10. "How Much Rest Do You Really Need?," Escape Haven, escapehaven.com/2022/09/benefits-of-rest.
11. Often attributed to Zig Ziglar.
12. Google Dictionary, "excellence," google.com/search?q=excellence+def.

CHAPTER 7: EATING WELL, MOVING MORE, SLEEPING SOUNDLY

1. Craig Groeschel, *Think Ahead: 7 Decisions You Can Make Today for the God-Honoring Life You Want Tomorrow* (Zondervan, 2024), 1–14.
2. "Healthy Eating Plate," The Nutrition Source, January 2023, nutritionsource.hsph.harvard.edu/healthy-eating-plate.
3. Julia Malacoff, "Eat More to Lose Weight: Why You Could Be Sabotaging Your Weight-Loss Efforts," Shape, September 8, 2024, shape.com/weight-loss/management/why-eating-more-secret-losing-weight.
4. Lizzie Streit, "What Are Macronutrients? All You Need to Know," Healthline, updated July 28, 2025, healthline.com/nutrition/what-are-macronutrients.
5. Kris Gunnars, "10 Science-Backed Reasons to Eat More Protein," Healthline, updated February 18, 2025, healthline.com/nutrition/10-reasons-to-eat-more-protein; Gavin Van De Walle, "9 Important Functions of Protein in Your Body," Healthline, updated February 15, 2023, healthline.com/nutrition/functions-of-protein; Ralph M. Trüeb, "'Let Food Be Thy Medicine': Value of Nutritional Treatment for Hair Loss," *International Journal of Trichology* 13, no. 6 (2021): 1–3, doi.org/10.4103/ijt.ijt_124_20.
6. Markham Heid, "Protect Your Health with the Right Dietary

Fats," MD Anderson Cancer Center, June 2015, mdandersoncellresearch.org/publications/focused-on-health/FOH-dietary-fats.h15-1589835.html; "Healthy Fats," Healthy UC Davis, healthy.ucdavis.edu/eating-well/nourish-labels/healthy-fats.

7. "Carbohydrates," Cleveland Clinic, updated March 8, 2024, my.clevelandclinic.org/health/articles/15416-carbohydrates; "Conquer Your Carb Confusion," American Diabetes Association, diabetes.org/food-nutrition/understanding-carbs/conquer-your-carbs; "Carbohydrates: How Carbs Fit into a Healthy Diet," Mayo Clinic, January 24, 2025, mayoclinic.org/healthy-lifestyle/nutrition-and-healthy-eating/in-depth/carbohydrates/art-20045705.
8. "Dietary Fiber: Essential for a Healthy Diet," Mayo Clinic, December 11, 2024, mayoclinic.org/healthy-lifestyle/nutrition-and-healthy-eating/in-depth/fiber/art-20043983; "Carbohydrates," Cleveland Clinic; Yang He et al., "Effects of Dietary Fiber on Human Health," *Food Science and Human Wellness* 11, no. 1 (2022): 1–10, doi.org/10.1016/j.fshw.2021.07.001; Faezeh Saghafian et al., "Consumption of Dietary Fiber in Relation to Psychological Disorders in Adults," *Frontiers in Psychiatry* 12 (2021), doi.org/10.3389/fpsyt.2021.587468.
9. Waseem Khalid et al., "Functional Constituents of Plant-Based Foods Boost Immunity Against Acute and Chronic Disorders," *Open Life Sciences* 17, no. 1 (2022): 1075–93, doi.org/10.1515/biol-2022-0104; Autumn Enloe, "The 13 Healthiest Leafy Green Vegetables," Healthline, updated February 15, 2024, healthline.com/nutrition/leafy-green-vegetables; Celia Vimont, "36 Fabulous Foods to Boost Eye Health," American Academy of Ophthalmology, November 21, 2024, aao.org/eye-health/tips-prevention/fabulous-foods-your-eyes; Lin Yan, "Dark Green Leafy Vegetables," USDA, updated September 11, 2023, ars.usda.gov/plains-area/gfnd/gfhnrc/docs/news-articles/2013/dark-green-leafy-vegetables; "Eating for Energy: Foods That Fight Fatigue," Cleveland Clinic, June 21, 2024, health.clevelandclinic.org/foods-that-give-you-energy; "Nour-

ish Your Skin from the Inside Out: Why Healthy Eating Is Key to Skin Health," Dallas Associated Dermatologists, October 28, 2024, dallasassocderm.com/nourish-your-skin-from-the-inside-out-why-healthy-eating-is-key-to-skin-health.

10. "The Fab Four," Be Well by Kelly LeVeque, bewellbykelly.com/pages/fab-four.
11. Shishira Sreenivas, "What Is Intuitive Eating?," WebMD, April 21, 2023, webmd.com/diet/what-is-intuitive-eating.
12. "Exercise: 7 Benefits of Regular Physical Activity," Mayo Clinic, August 26, 2023, mayoclinic.org/healthy-lifestyle/fitness/in-depth/exercise/art-20048389.
13. "Good Sleep? Good Job! How Sleep Health Boosts Productivity," National Sleep Foundation, March 5, 2025, thensf.org/sleep-and-productivity; "The Psychology of Sleep: Why Is Sleep Important for Our Mental and Physical Health?," Insights Psychology, October 29, 2024, insightspsychology.org/psychology-of-sleep-mental-and-physical-benefits.
14. "The Psychology of Sleep," Insights Psychology.
15. "Study Reveals the Face of Sleep Deprivation," American Academy of Sleep Medicine, August 30, 2013, aasm.org/study-reveals-the-face-of-sleep-deprivation; "Sleep Quality May Impact Skin," AASM Sleep Education, July 24, 2013, sleepeducation.org/sleep-quality-may-impact-skin.
16. "The Psychology of Sleep," Insights Psychology.
17. "The Psychology of Sleep," Insights Psychology.
18. "The Connection Between Sleep, Diabetes, and Obesity," Yale Medicine, March 13, 2023, yalemedicine.org/news/sleep-diabetes-and-obesity; Rebecca Joy Stanborough, "How Does Cortisol Affect Your Sleep?," Healthline, July 10, 2020, healthline.com/health/cortisol-and-sleep; Ida Szataniak and Kacper Packi, "Melatonin as the Missing Link Between Sleep Deprivation and Immune Dysregulation: A Narrative Review," *International Journal of Molecular Sciences* 26, no. 14 (2025), doi.org/10.3390/ijms26146731.
19. "The Psychology of Sleep," Insights Psychology.
20. Lieke ten Brummelhuis, "Why Working Long Hours Hurts

Your Work Performance," *Forbes,* January 8, 2025, forbes.com/sites/lieketenbrummelhuis/2025/01/08/why-working-long-hours-hurts-your-work-performance.

21. Christopher Drake et al., "Caffeine Effects on Sleep Taken 0, 3, or 6 Hours Before Going to Bed," *Journal of Clinical Sleep Medicine* 9, no. 11 (2013), doi.org/10.5664/jcsm.3170; Carissa Gardiner et al., "The Effect of Caffeine on Subsequent Sleep: A Systematic Review and Meta-Analysis," *Sleep Medicine Reviews* 69 (2023), doi.org/10.1016/j.smrv.2023.101764.
22. Lauren Fountain, "Caffeine and Sleep," Sleep Foundation, updated July 16, 2025, sleepfoundation.org/nutrition/caffeine-and-sleep.
23. Kristeen Cherney, "How Long Does Caffeine Stay in Your System?," Healthline, updated November 7, 2018, healthline.com/health/how-long-does-caffeine-last#how-long-symptoms-last.
24. "Chamomile vs Lavender: Which Herb Is Best for Relaxation?," Bluestem Botanicals, February 16, 2025, bluestembotanicals.com/blogs/news/chamomile-vs-lavender-which-herb-is-best-for-relaxation.
25. Jay Vera Summer, "Using Magnesium for Better Sleep," Sleep Foundation, updated March 27, 2024, sleepfoundation.org/magnesium#benefits-of-magnesium-for-sleep.
26. Rob Newsom, "Blue Light: What It Is and How It Affects Sleep," Sleep Foundation, updated July 11, 2025, sleepfoundation.org/bedroom-environment/blue-light; Lucy Bryan, "Melatonin: Usage, Side Effects, and Safety," Sleep Foundation, updated July 10, 2025, sleepfoundation.org/melatonin.
27. "Screen Use Disrupts Precious Sleep Time," National Sleep Foundation, March 13, 2022, thensf.org/screen-use-disrupts-precious-sleep-time.
28. "Water: Essential for Your Body," Mayo Clinic Health System, September 29, 2022, mayoclinichealthsystem.org/hometown-health/speaking-of-health/water-essential-to-your-body-video; Joe Leech, "7 Science-Based Health Benefits of Drinking Enough Water," Healthline, updated March 8, 2023, healthline

.com/nutrition/7-health-benefits-of-water; Lucy Bryan, "Surprising Ways Hydration Affects Your Sleep," Sleep Foundation, updated July 16, 2025, sleepfoundation.org/nutrition/hydration-and-sleep.

29. "Dehydration," Cleveland Clinic, June 5, 2023, my.clevelandclinic.org/health/diseases/9013-dehydration; Kathryn Watson, "What Does It Mean When Dehydration Becomes Long-Term and Serious?," Healthline, updated April 24, 2023, healthline.com/health/chronic-dehydration#symptoms; Carolyn Farnsworth, "What to Know About Dehydration and Joint Pain," Medical News Today, November 16, 2022, medicalnewstoday.com/articles/dehydration-joint-pain; "The Cognitive Effects of Proper Hydration," Sqwincher, osha.gov/sites/default/files/2023BeatTheHeatWinners/Contest_Innovative_Kent Precision_CognitiveEffectsHydration.pdf.
30. Kara-Marie Hall, "How Much Water Should You Drink Every Day?," GoodRx, updated December 16, 2024, goodrx.com/well-being/diet-nutrition/how-much-water-should-i-drink-daily.
31. "The Set Point Theory and How It Will Change the Way We Think About Weight Loss," Weight Loss Center of the North Shore, January 20, 2023, weightlosscenterns.com/weight-loss-resources/2023/1/11/the-set-point-theory-and-how-it-will-change-the-way-we-think-about-weight-loss.

CHAPTER 8: BEARING THE WEIGHT OF WAITING

1. *The Shack,* directed by Stuart Hazeldine (Lionsgate, 2017).
2. Stephen R. Covey, *The 7 Habits of Highly Effective People: Powerful Lessons in Personal Change* (Free Press, 2004), 83, 88.

About the Author

Ashley Hetherington is an author, speaker, content creator, Jesus lover, and bookworm. She's also the founder of the Honey Scoop, a platform that encourages and equips young women to grow their faith and reach their full potential in God. She has a passion for connecting with young women about the struggles of young adult life, especially with those who want to know the Word of God and let His truth transform their lives. Through her writing and speaking, as well as her membership program, the Tree—an online community focused on growing closer to God and reading the Bible—Ashley is a faith leader for young women.

About the Type

This book was set in Sabon, a typeface designed by the well-known German typographer Jan Tschichold (1902–74). Sabon's design is based upon the original letter forms of sixteenth-century French type designer Claude Garamond and was created specifically to be used for three sources: foundry type for hand composition, Linotype, and Monotype. Tschichold named his typeface for the famous Frankfurt typefounder Jacques Sabon (c. 1520–80).

Also from bestselling author

ASHLEY HETHERINGTON

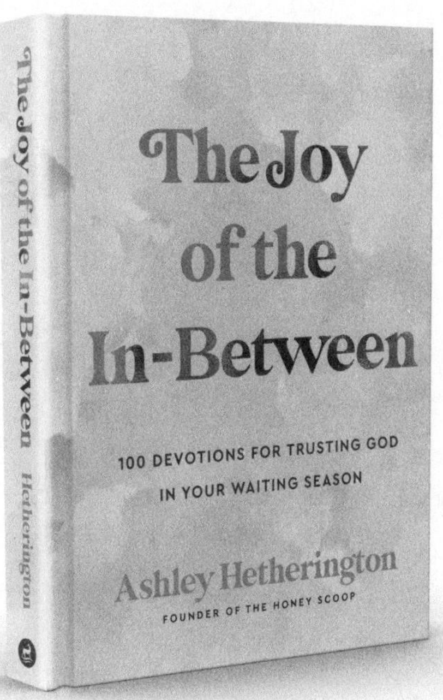

You have big dreams, but you're waiting on God for something: the career, the spouse, or maybe the life you've been praying for. But today is important too.

Discover how you can experience more joy, purpose, and trust in God exactly where you are, and learn to embrace *The Joy of the In-Between*.

Learn more about Ashley's books at waterbrookmultnomah.com